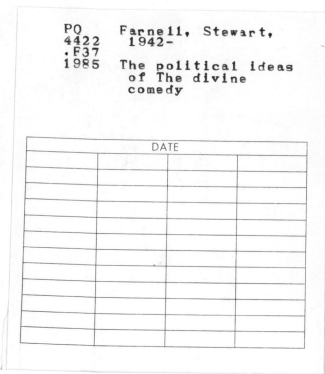

# THE POLITICAL IDEAS OF THE DIVINE COMEDY

## An Introduction

### Stewart Farnell

UNIVERSITY
PRESS OF
AMERICA

LANHAM • NEW YORK • LONDON

## ACKNOWLEDGMENTS

This work was made possible by the grant of a sabbatical leave by Saint Thomas More College of the University of Saskatchewan, and by a grant from the Social Sciences and Humanities Research Council of Canada. The Library of the Pontifical Institute of Mediaeval Studies at the University of Saint Michael's College, and the Robarts Library of the University of Toronto both gave ready access to their collections. Jene Porter, Margot King and David Farmer read the manuscript and provided valuable criticism. Silvine Marbury helped edit the final draft and made many helpful suggestions.

# TABLE OF CONTENTS

# INTRODUCTION

Since The Divine Comedy is an allegory, its meaning is not always readily apparent--it needs to be deciphered. This book is intended for those who, reading the poem in English translation, seek a guide to its political ideas. It is directed to newcomers to The Divine Comedy, whether they be students in classes in political theory, comparative literature, history, literary criticism, classics in translation, or members of the general reading public.

While Dante is remembered chiefly as a poet rather than a political theorist, The Divine Comedy cannot be understood without some knowledge of his political ideas. For Dante, politics, private life, religion, and scholarship were not isolated fields of endeavor but parts of a larger Whole, the order of the universe centered in God its creator. Seeing political life as part of the greater Whole, he deliberately chose as characters for his wonderful poem not only popes, poets, saints, and sinners, but philosophers, politicians, emperors, and soldiers as well. The threads of Dante's political thinking are essential parts of the splendid tapestry of The Divine Comedy.

Chapter 1 of this book briefly considers Dante's life, his politically formative experiences, and his other political writings. Chapters 2 through 5 present The Divine Comedy's political ideas in the context of the poem's unequalled vision of the greater Whole. Chapter 6 contends that these ideas are not haphazard, but fall into a pattern, making them a coherent body of political thought. Finally, Chapter 7 assesses the merit of the political teaching of one of the great creative achievements of western civilization, Dante's Divine Comedy.

# Chapter 1

## DANTE

Why did Dante deliberately weave political ideas into the fabric of <u>The Divine Comedy</u>? What events impelled him to use his great poem to proclaim a political teaching? This chapter looks at the experiences that shaped Dante's political convictions.

Dante's political ideas were the product of his experience. He participated actively in the politics of his native Florence, but the perpetual turmoil he found there ultimately disillusioned him. Aware of the disorder around him, he asked some fundamental political questions. Is there a right ordering of public affairs? If so, what is it? What stands in the way of its achievement? Can it be accomplished despite such obstacles? Dante also questioned the relation of political life to the greater Whole. As he grew in spiritual awareness he became more and more conscious that the universe has its origin beyond time and space, in God. Of what value are political doings, political men, and political lives viewed against the backdrop of the infinite and the eternal? These questions quickened Dante's thinking. Their answers he incorporated in the mature fruit of his creative genius, <u>The Divine Comedy</u>.

Dante was born in 1265. His family, though neither wealthy nor very aristocratic, was nevertheless of the nobility. Educated as befitted a young Florentine gentleman, Dante was prepared for both his poetic vocation and his civic responsibilities. His family belonged to the ruling Guelf party. The Guelfs professed to be supporters of the popes against the emperors, and defenders of the rights and independence of the Italian cities. The Florentine Guelfs were, however, primarily concerned with retaining power in their native city, and with extending their influence, and that of Florence, throughout Tuscany. The Guelf's Ghibelline opponents, nominal supporters of the emperors and the feudal aristocracy, were equally intent upon ruling Florence and Tuscany, and equally willing to make whatever bargains and accommodations were necessary to do so.

But the bitter power struggle between Guelfs and Ghibellines did not immediately command Dante's attention. Early in life he was dazzled by the beauty and grace of Beatrice Portinari, a young Florentine of his acquaintance. In her he saw not just a girl of rare and glorious beauty, but a revelation of God. The wonder and awe he felt awakened his imagination, and led to the rapid development of his poetic talents. While the young Dante was not unaware of civic affairs, his attention centered on Beatrice and on poetry.

The orderly unfolding of Dante's life was abruptly shattered when Beatrice died in 1290. Out of his ensuing inner turmoil Dante created a remarkable early work, the Vita Nuova. The Vita Nuova deals with love, yet at the same time the heavenward aspiration of its young author is evident. The Beatrice of this work is more than a beauty and a wonder to Dante, she is a channel by which his love ascends to Heaven. The great Danteist Charles Singleton writes that "one knows at the end of the Vita Nuova, that, as a theory of love, it was based on reaching Heaven.... The whole work, from its first words, may be said to be aiming at Heaven--which is reached in its last words."[1] The Vita Nuova thus discloses the faint beginnings of the spiritual awareness that characterizes The Divine Comedy.

Beatrice's death shook Dante to the core. In time, however, he found consolation in philosophy and distraction in politics. Both endeavors excited his interest, broadened his horizons, and showed him their limitations. Eventually he found them incomplete without a vision of the Whole to put each in its proper place and illuminate its significance. Dante came to this conclusion only gradually, as his initial enthusiasms were refined by experience and reflection. His first efforts in these fields, however, were marked by boldness and enthusiasm. To console himself for the loss of Beatrice, he read Boethius and Cicero, and these whetted his appetite for further knowledge. He threw himself into the study of philosophy and quickly acquired a considerable store of learning. Dante's scholarship had its origin in his need for consolation, and his enthusiasm for learning drew much of its nourishment from the conviction that philosophy could provide the guidance he needed to live an active life, despite the loss of Beatrice.

----------

1. An Essay on the Vita Nuova (Cambridge: Harvard University Press, 1949), p. 101.

The practical side of Dante's nature showed itself in 1295, when he began to play an active role in Florentine politics. Maintaining his connection with the dominant Guelph party, Dante rose to occupy important posts in the government of Florence. The Guelfs, securely in control in Florence, quarreled among themselves, dividing into two hostile factions, the Whites and the Blacks. Dante sided with the Whites. In November of 1301 the Whites were forcibly suppressed by the Blacks, aided by the wily Pope Boniface VIII and by twelve hundred troops led by the brother of the King of France. Dante, a prominent White, found himself exiled from the city of which he had recently been a leading citizen.

The blow hurt. Dante was a proud man. Like many political men he sought appreciation and fame, not abuse, exile, and a sentence of death should he dare return to his native city. For a time he threw in his lot with other Florentine exiles, both White Guelf and Ghibelline. He soon broke with his companions, however. He was not to devote his life to the schemes and dreams of embittered exiles. Unlike Machiavelli, for example, he lacked an all-consuming fascination with politics. Karl Vossler notes that

> Dante tested himself and was tested, in statesmanship, but with no great success. He had ambition, but not unconditional love for political life. He could not be wholly absorbed by it, would not, had occasion demanded, have risked his soul for it.[2]

Dante's learned much from his years in Florentine politics. His eyes were opened to a wider field of action than that afforded by the worlds of scholarship and romantic love. Dean Church, in his classic essay on Dante, asserts that

> it was the factions of Florence which made Dante a great poet. ...he learned in the bitter feuds of Italy not to trifle; they opened to his view, and he had an eye to see, the true springs and abysses of this mortal life--motives and passions stronger

----------

2. _Medieval Culture: An Introduction to Dante and His Times_, trans. W. C. Lawton (New York: Ungar, 1929), I, 332.

3

than lovers' sentiments, evils beyond the consolations of Boethius and Cicero.[3]

Dante never set foot in Florence again. During the decades of his banishment he lived in the households of noble rulers and patrons, who were happy to have the foremost poet of the age adorn their courts. One such patron and friend was Can Grande della Scalla, the lord of Verona, to whom Dante dedicated the _Paradiso_. Dante undertook diplomatic missions for some of these rulers. His travels showed him that disorder in public life was not unique to Florence--tumult and turbulence convulsed most of Italy. Reflecting on this disorder, Dante sought its source.

Dante's early thoughts on the sad state of Italian politics are recorded in the _Banquet_.[4] Composed in the early years of his exile (1304-1308), the _Banquet_ was never finished. Its subject is not politics, yet political questions do arise in it, indicating the importance such questions held for its author. Here, in this preliminary work, we see Dante's political ideas beginning to take shape.

The _Banquet_ grew out of Dante's enthusiasm for philosophy. Its purpose is to share the fruits of his philosophic labors with people who lack the time to pursue such studies themselves. It celebrates philosophy's capacity to bring fulfillment to the active life, the life lived by rulers, merchants, soldiers and all who are caught up in the hustle and bustle of the world's affairs. Philosophy, Dante holds, particularly Aristotle's philosophy, provides the knowledge of moral virtue that enables men to act rightly and thereby achieve happiness.[5]

Philosophy can teach virtue, but few men appreciate its worth. In their fierce, wilful self-seeking most men have no time for philosophy and little regard for moral virtue. Herein lies the source of Italy's

----------

3. Richard William Church, _Dante. An Essay_ (London: Macmillan, 1878), p. 8. This essay was first published in the _Christian Remembrancer_, January, 1850.

4. _Convivio_ in Italian.

5. _The Convivio_, trans. P. H. Wicksteed (4th ed.; London: Dent, 1924), IV. 6.

4

woes and the justification for the authority of the Empire. The Emperor restrains men's self-seeking and steers them in the direction of virtuous action. He maintains peace among those who would break it and upholds the law that habituates men to act rightly. He is "the rider of the human will". But in Italy the Emperor's authority is not upheld, and

> how that horse [the human will] courses over the plain without the rider is manifest enough; and especially in wretched Italy which, without any mediator at all, has been abandoned to her own direction.[6]

If men are to achieve the felicity of the active life, the guidance of the Empire is essential. Without such guidance, men's lives are spent in suffering, experiencing the ravages of the politics of unbridled will. Dante's experience of Italy's turbulent politics thus led him to part company with the Empire-hating Guelfs.

If the Emperor is to help men gain felicity, he must help them practice the moral virtues. Otherwise, his guidance will be of no avail. The Empire and philosophy thus need each other; they are separate but mutually dependent authorities. The Emperor needs the knowledge of moral virtue discovered by "the supreme philosopher" (Aristotle) to guide him in guiding others. The philosopher needs the Emperor to "still the disorderliness of men" and give practical application to his knowledge of how the life of action can be a life of fulfillment.[7]

By the time Dante wrote the Banquet he clearly had grasped the idea of Empire, the idea of a universal monarchy, a world government that could bring peace and order to the tumultuous, strife-ridden political realm. But the fragmented and unsystematic treatment the idea of Empire here receives suggests that Dante had yet to work out its full implications, and integrate it into the main body of his thinking; it was still new to him. Born and bred a Guelf, hailing from Ghibelline-hating Florence, it took him time to digest the idea of Empire.

----------

6. Convivio, IV. 9.

7. Convivio, IV. 6.

The _Banquet_ was never finished. We do not know why. We know little about the details of Dante's life. Some scholars hold that he abandoned his lesser works to undertake his masterpiece, _The Divine Comedy_. Others believe he dropped everything to write _Monarchy_, the work which systematically expounds the idea of Empire.[8] In any case, a new and exciting phase in his life was soon to begin.

Political events were taking an encouraging turn for this convert to the idea of Empire. Dante watched enthusiastically as the Emperor Henry VII attempted to reassert Imperial authority in Italy. His excitement is evident in three letters he wrote between 1310 and 1313. He tried to aid Henry as best he could, raising his pen in eloquent support of the Emperor's cause. Dante's first letter is to the temporal rulers of Italy. It heralds the Emperor's coming as the dawning of a new era, a time of peace and justice for Italy. As the Empire is pre-ordained by God, Henry should be received as Italy's God-appointed ruler. The next letter is addressed to the citizens of Florence, the foremost Guelf power in north Italy, and the leader in opposing Henry by force of arms. Rebellion against the Empire is rebellion against the will of God, and leads only to destruction, Dante thunders. The third letter is to the Emperor Henry himself. It exhorts him to quickly crush Florence, which Dante identifies as the center of Italian resistance to Henry's expedition.

All three letters demonstrate Dante's intense interest in political affairs. The letter to the Florentines, in its early, more moderate passages, shows the direction of his thinking. Providence, he says, "committed to the Holy Roman Empire the govern-ance of human affairs, to the end that mankind might repose in the peace of so powerful a protection, and everywhere, as nature demands, might live as citizens of an ordered world." Proof for this is found not only

----------

8. The date of _Monarchy_'s composition is the subject of disagreement; some scholars place it at the end of Dante's life, after the completion of _The Divine Comedy_ (1319-1321); others attribute it to the period of the Emperor Henry's Italian expedition, (1310-1313). For a brief treatment of the controversy see George Holmes, "Dante and the Popes," in Cecil Grayson, ed., _The World of Dante_ (Oxford: Oxford University Press, 1980), pp. 29-30.

in Scripture and in the discoveries of the ancient philosophers, but also in contemporary experience. Identifying the Holy Roman Empire of his day with the Empire of ancient Rome, he writes:

> When the throne of Augustus [the throne of the Empire] is vacant, the whole universe goes out of course, the helmsman and rowers slumber in the ship of Peter [the Church], and unhappy Italy, forsaken and abandoned to private control, and bereft of all public guidance, is tossed with such buffeting of winds and waves as no words can describe, nay as even the Italians in their woe can scarce measure with their tears.[9]

This assertion of the importance of the Emperorship echoes the **Banquet**'s statement of the same idea. But a new element has been added. The "ship of Peter," the Church, now commands Dante's attention. Dante's recognition of the significance of the Church is paralleled by a growing consciousness of the larger setting of political life. These letters foreshadow what will be a major theme of The Divine Comedy, the contention that the political order is part of the order of God's universe, the order of the Whole.

Dante's hopes for an immediate revival of Imperial authority were soon dashed. Opposed by King Henry IV of France and Pope Clement V, the Emperor Henry died in his unsuccessful attempt to bring Italy under control. Italy remained disordered. But Henry's expedition left its mark on Dante's thinking. The revival of the Empire was henceforth no abstract idea to Dante; it was a real possibility.

The world's disorder can be remedied. This belief was to remain with Dante to the end of his days. It led him to systematically expound the idea of a universal Empire in his treatise Monarchy. Monarchy aims first to prove the need for a universal Empire, second to demonstrate the legitimacy of the Roman Empire as the divinely ordained universal monarchy, and third to show that the Emperor holds his temporal authority quite independent of the Pope. Each of these questions

----------

9. Letter VI, in Epistolae: the Letters of Dante, trans. Paget Toynbee (2nd ed.; Oxford: Clarendon Press, 1920), p. 77.

7

was controverted in Dante's day. On each point Dante supports the Emperor against those who would diminish his authority.

Each book of the Monarchy takes up one of these points. To show the need for a universal Empire, Book I builds a novel argument from what were familiar premises. All associations, Dante asserts, are directed toward the achievement of some goal. From the familiar assertion that different associations have different ends, Dante draws a conclusion that was new to medieval thinking. If different associations have different ends,[10] then the human species must have its own distinct end.

> The end toward which the individual's life
> is directed is different from that of the
> family community; the village has one end,
> the city another and the kingdom another;
> and best of all there is the end that the
> eternal God has established for the whole
> human race by means of his art.[11]

For Dante the human race is one association, one commonwealth. Like any association, it must have its own end. What is this end? It must be found in the distinctive capacity of the human species, for the proper functioning of any being is its ultimate end, the end for which it has been made by the Creator. The distinctive function of mankind is the capacity to grow in knowledge, to use what the medievals called the possible intellect. Animals have no intellect at all, just sensation. Angels, possessing immediate and direct knowledge, lack the potential to grow in knowledge. The capacity to grow in knowledge is thus the unique property of human beings. And as the capacity to grow

----------

10. The concept of a universal civilization with its own end had existed in other civilizations, however. See Eric Voegelin, The Ecumenic Age, Volume IV of Order in History (Baton Rouge: Louisiana State University Press, 1974), pp. 135-145.

11. Monarchy I. 1. Quotations are from the translation of Donald Nicholl in Monarchy and Three Political Letters (London, Weidenfeld and Nicholson, 1954). Where necessary Nicholl's translation has been updated to reflect Ricci's more recent and authoritative edition of the Latin text.

in knowledge cannot be exhausted by any one person, it is only mankind collectively which can fulfill this distinctive capacity. To grow in knowledge is thus the proper function of mankind, and therefore its end.[12]

To achieve its goal mankind requires peace. As individuals find that by sitting quietly they are best able to grow in wisdom, so mankind is best able to fulfill its collective end of growing in knowledge in the quiet, the tranquility of peace.".[13] The role of the Empire is to bring about that peace.

The idea that the entire human species is one association with its own proper end was most convenient for Dante. It served as the foundation of a powerful argument for the necessity of a universal Empire. If the entire human race is one association having a natural, God-ordained end, and if peace is required for the attainment of that goal, then the Empire, as guardian of the peace, is the necessary means to the end. As such, the Empire too is natural and ordained by God.

Book I contains an abundance of subsidiary arguments, all leading to the conclusion that a universal monarchy is necessary for the world to be peaceful and well ordered. Chapter 15, in a passage that recalls Dante's thinking in the Banquet, holds that concord among men requires that their wills be united. Such unity does not occur spontaneously; since men's wills are "influenced by their adolescent and seductive delights," they "are in need of a director." The Emperor is this director. He provides the single will needed to bring about unity and concord. He does not impose uniformity, however, nor does the Empire's existence do away with the need for regional governments. The Empire's function is to maintain peace among the rulers of different states, and to see that the universal law (based on what all men have in common) is everywhere upheld. Regional and municipal laws, however, must be adapted to the needs of different peoples and different climates. This is the responsibility of local governments.[14]

----------

12. Monarchy I. 3.

13. Monarchy I. 4.

14. See Monarchy I. 14.

Book I concludes with an audacious argument. Dante asserts that Christ's choosing to come into the world during the reign of the Emperor Augustus demonstrates divine approval of the Empire, an essential institution in a well-ordered world.[15] A cognate argument occurs in Book II.

Book II asks if it was by right that the Roman people acquired their Empire. As a Guelf, Dante once believed that the Romans had gained their empire by armed force rather than by right.[16] Now, by contrast, he argues that God's hand lay behind Rome's acquisition of her Empire; the Empire rules by the will of God, and therefore by right. Book II's most interesting argument comes at its close. Dante claims that Christ, by allowing Himself to be crucified by the Roman authorities, recognized the validity of the Empire.[17] Dante starts from the premise that Adam's sin (ie. the sin of mankind) was punished in Christ's death on the cross. For Christ's sacrifice to have been a valid punishment, the Empire's authority had to be legitimate. If Rome's power was not based on right, it could not have justly punished Christ; Christ's death would not have been a punishment, which is inflicted by right, but a mere injury done without right. If the Empire lacked authority it could not punish. If it did not punish, Christ did not atone. But Christ did atone, hence the Empire's authority must be legitimate.

Book III seeks to demonstrate that the Emperor possesses his authority independent of the Pope. This is a necessary step for Dante. After all, the idea that the Popes possessed complete temporal as well as spiritual authority on earth was common in Dante's time. Indeed, his arch-foe, Pope Boniface VIII, vigorously asserted this view in his bull Unam Sanctam. Dante's own position thus far is compatible with the view that the universal Monarch ruling by right is none other than the Pope. Thus Book III begins by refuting arguments for the supremacy of the Popes in temporal affairs.

----------

15. Monarchy I. 16.

16. Monarchy II. 1.

17. Monarchy II. 10.

Some of these arguments are found in <u>The Divine Comedy</u>, especially those concerning the Popes' powers of binding and loosing, and the Church's capacity for acquiring temporal wealth and power. The binding and loosing argument is used by Boniface in <u>Unam Sanctam</u>. He cites the Gospel of Saint Matthew, wherein Christ tells Peter, the first Pope: "I give you the keys to the kingdom, and whatsoever you shall have bound on earth shall be bound in heaven; and whatsoever you shall have loosed on earth shall be loosed in heaven." The Pope's claim to wield complete power is based on the words of Christ Himself. Dante disagrees. The Pope's power is not unlimited. The Pontiff cannot divorce people, nor can he absolve the impenitent. This, Dante presumes, all his readers will accept. Since the Pope's power <u>is</u> limited, Christ's statement does not grant absolute power. What, then, does it grant? Dante points to its context. Christ says to Peter "I give you the keys to the kingdom" meaning "I shall make you custodian of the kingdom of heaven."[18] Peter's power thus is spiritual, not temporal. It relates to keeping the keys to the kingdom of heaven, not to the exercise of worldly authority.

Another of Boniface's arguments concerns the Donation of Constantine, the Emperor Constantine's alleged gift of his temporal authority in the West to the Church. Dante does not challenge the historical evidence for the Donation. Instead, he holds the Emperor had no right to surrender his prerogatives, and the Church no right to accept them. The very nature of the Empire as the universal temporal monarchy precludes its division. Even if Constantine, misled by his devotion to the Church, did try to donate temporal authority in the West to the Pope, he had no right to do so. Just as the Emperor has no right to relinquish this authority, the Church cannot rightfully hold title to it. To buttress his view that the Church must eschew temporal gifts, Dante quotes Matthew: "Possess not gold nor silver, nor money in your girdles, nor purse for your journey." The Church, he holds, may accept donations, "as administrator of the fruits for the benefits of the Church and the poor of Christ",[19] but it cannot accept outright ownership. Applied to the Donation

----------

18. <u>Monarchy</u> III. 8.

19. <u>Monarchy</u> III. 10.

supreme proprietorship of temporal authority. The Emperor retains his authority and is not subordinate to the Pope in temporal affairs. Because of the natures of Empire and Church, even the Donation of Constantine cannot make the Pope the temporal superior of the Emperor.

The most interesting part of Monarchy comes at the end of Book III. Having refuted to his satisfaction arguments for papal supremacy, Dante states his own views on the relation of Emperor to Pope. He carefully builds to the conclusion that the Emperor receives his authority directly from God rather than from God via the Pope. Pope and Emperor are coordinate authorities, each supreme within his own sphere of activity.

Dante begins by asserting that man is a unique creature, one who unites in his nature the opposite qualities of corruptibility and incorruptibility. Looked at in terms of both his essential constituents, body and soul, man is corruptible, since the body dies, and the body and soul compound is dissolved. But looked at in terms of his soul, man is incorruptible, for his soul is immortal. Every nature has its ultimate goal, but since man's nature is twofold, man has two ultimate goals, "duo ultima."[20] One is his goal as a corruptible creature, other as an incorruptible one.[21] Each of these ends has its own attendant felicity.

> Unerring Providence has therefore set man to attain two goals; the first is happiness in this life, which consists in the exercise of his own powers and is typified by the earthly paradise; the second is the happiness of eternal life, which consists in the enjoyment of the divine countenance (which man cannot attain to of his own power but only by aid of divine illumination) and is typified by the heavenly paradise.[22]

----------

20. The individual person, not the human race as a whole, has two ends. The human race retains the end attributed it in Book I, to grow in knowledge.

21. Monarchy III. 15.

22. Monarchy III. 15.

In arguing that man has two ultimate goals, not one, Dante denies the medieval assumption that man has only one goal which is in any sense ultimate, his goal as a spiritual being. In saying that man also has a final goal as an earthly, temporal creature, Dante breaks important new ground.

How do men achieve their dual goals? Monarchy teaches that man's two goals are attained by different means. One goal, temporal felicity, is attained through the exercise of the moral and intellectual virtues discovered by philosophy, especially Aristotle's philosophy. The other, eternal happiness, is arrived at "by means of spiritual teaching (which transcends human reason) in so far as we exercise the theological virtues of faith, hope and charity."[23]

Philosophy and spiritual teaching are of no use to those who reject them, however, and human beings are all too prone to do so. Accordingly, man has been given two guides, Emperor and Pope, each to direct him to one of his two ends. The Emperor places temporal power in the service of philosophical teaching. He helps free men from the "waves of alluring cupidity," from being dominated by their greedy appetites. He helps them know peace even within the boundaries of mortal existence. The Emperor's function to see that men enjoy peace and freedom "as they pass through the testing time of this world." To carry out this daunting task, God Himself chooses the Emperor. The Emperor "receives his authority directly, and without intermediary, from the source of all authority [God]."[24] The Emperor, though not subordinate to the Pope in temporal matters, still owes the spiritual Pontiff "reverence". As a devout Christian the Emperor should revere the Pope, not, certainly, as political overlord, but as spiritual teacher. This is an ingenious formula, though not without difficulties. Monarchy, however, does not address them.

Whatever its shortcomings, Monarchy is a significant work. The argument that mankind has a collective end requiring a universal Empire for its achievement is original. The argument that Christ recognized the legitimacy of the Empire by choosing to be born and to

----------

23. Monarchy III. 15.

24. Monarchy III. 15.

13

die under its authority is audacious. Finally, the distinction between man's natural end, attainable through the practice of the moral virtues (discovered by philosophy, and fostered by the power of the Emperor to uphold the law), and man's eternal end, attainable through the practice of the spiritual virtues (known through revelation, and proclaimed by the Church) provides grounds, conceptually at least, for excluding the Pope from the exercise of temporal power.

Dante expounds his political ideas in several works, one of which is The Divine Comedy. Its ideas, like those of his other writings, were shaped by their author's experiences. While writing The Divine Comedy Dante travelled in Italy, seeing again and again the warfare and convulsion that beset his homeland. The poem's political ideas were also influenced by the failure of Henry VII's Italian expedition. This unhappy episode strengthened Dante's opposition to the the swollen power of the kings of France, and his antagonism to the interventions of the Papacy in secular affairs.

While Dante was writing The Divine Comedy both Emperor and Pope were being overshadowed by the growing power of independent states. France in particular had grown extremely strong. The conflict between Church and Empire was giving way to a struggle among sovereign states. The old medieval world, united, in principle at least, in the universal institutions of Church and Empire, was passing away. Dante understood these developments within his own intellectual framework. While The Divine Comedy has some harsh words for French monarchs, it attributes the world's ills chiefly to the corruption of the Church. The Church, by setting itself up as a rival to the temporal power of the Empire, keeps the Empire from carrying out its appointed task; the weakness of the Empire in turn prevents it from restraining the excesses of temporal kings. Consequently, national monarchies wax in power, Empire and Church wane, and the world goes astray.

Dante's rejection of ecclesiastical intervention in temporal affairs by no means entailed a rejection of the Church's spiritual message. Indeed, The Divine Comedy chastizes the Church for neglecting to proclaim that message. The Church's preoccupation with worldly wealth and power not only subverts the Empire and disorders the political world, it also diverts the Church from its own crucial mission.

14

The Divine Comedy reveals Dante's deep appreciation of the larger context of political life. Politics is only part of the Whole, and a rather small part at that. Of what import is public life when seen from such an exalted spiritual perspective? For Dante, it was of considerable importance. Convinced that the world's disorder impedes the quest for spiritual salvation, a disorder caused in part by political wrongs and requiring political action to set it right, he could hardly completely disparage political life. Instead, he achieved a view of the Whole which recognized its majesty and wonder without devaluing the worth of its parts. His consciousness of the goodness and pervasiveness of God led him to an awareness of the worth of all of God's creation, including political life.

Thus, while spiritual realities mattered greatly to Dante as he wrote The Divine Comedy, political life was not forgotten. Indeed, political concerns were in the forefront of his attention to the end of his life. He died in 1321, of a fever contracted while on a diplomatic mission from Ravenna to Venice.

# Chapter 2

## THE DIVINE COMEDY

Dante's life experience stimulated his political thinking and drove him to set forth his conclusions. This chapter looks at one context in which he chose to publish his ideas, The Divine Comedy. Two important aspects of the poem confront those who seek its political teaching. One is its holistic perspective, which raises the question of the significance of political life in light of the greater Whole. The other is the poem's allegorical form, which has led scholars to develop special analytical tools with which to unlock its meaning.

Although many of the political ideas of The Divine Comedy are also found in Monarchy[1] an important difference of emphasis distinguishes these works. Monarchy's emphasis is predominantly, though not exclusively, secular; that of The Divine Comedy is more spiritual. Dean Church perceptively notes that Dante

> entered on his great poem, to shadow forth under the figure of his own conversion and purification, not merely how a single soul rises to its perfection, but how this visible world, in all its phases of nature, life, and society, is one with the invisible, which borders on it, actuates, accomplishes, and explains it.[2]

Unlike Monarchy, which is focused on a small part of the totality of God's creation, the Empire, The Divine Comedy's vision is broader. It encompasses the

----------

1. On the vexed question of the consistency of the Monarchy with The Divine Comedy see Allesandro Passerin d'Entrèves, Dante as a Political Thinker (Oxford: Clarendon Press, 1952), pp. 59-60; Dorothy Sayers, Introductory Papers on Dante (New York: Barnes and Noble, 1969, c. 1954), p. 113; U. Limentani, "Dante's Political Thought," in The Mind of Dante, ed. U. Limentani, (Cambridge: Cambridge University Press, 1965), p. 115.

2. Richard William Church, Dante, An Essay, p. 77.

Whole, both in respect to its parts and in respect to the totality that is more than the sum of its parts. It does not repudiate politics, but discovers and articulates the place of political life in the larger Whole.

Dante's appreciation of the Whole derives from his awareness of God's ubiquity. Dante sees man as part of the natural world, a world whose secrets are unfolded by ancient philosophy. This is the doctrine of the Banquet, but now, in The Divine Comedy, the natural world is emphatically God's world; the natural is integrated with the spiritual. No part of creation is beyond the embrace of the divine aspect.

The universe is a Whole, and God, its Creator, is its end as well as its beginning. Like other medieval thinkers, Dante saw in the universe an order and harmony that was directly attributable to its divine Maker.[3] The Divine Comedy is Dante's attempt to accurately represent that order. Charles Singleton says that Dante's poem, The Divine Comedy, is "an analogue to God's poem," the universe.[4] Joseph Mazzeo concurs. To him The Divine Comedy is "a microcosm of the universe," analogically reflecting the structural principles of the Whole.[5] The universe of The Divine Comedy is thus no arbitrary creation on Dante's part. It is a faithful attempt to represent poetically the true nature of existence.

The central principle, both of God's creation and Dante's Divine Comedy is order. Within the structure of the Whole, moral and political life have their own proper structures. The purpose of this order is to allow God's creatures to live in joyful harmony with their Creator. To attain temporal and eternal happiness, individual souls need to be rightly-ordered. For Church and Empire to help men attain these goals, they too must be ordered aright.

----------

3. See Singleton, Essay on the Vita Nuova, p. 46.

4. "Dante's Comedy: The Pattern at the Center," Romanic Review, XLII (1951), 117.

5. Medieval Cultural Tradition in Dante's "Comedy" (Ithaca, N.Y.: Cornell University Press), p. 2.

Disorder, indeed, is Dante's explanation of the ills of the world. Individuals and kingdoms are ruled by cupidity, by disordered love which values trivial goods like power, wealth and fame above virtue and spirituality. The prevalence of cupidity in the world is the source of man's misery, individual and social. God has harmoniously arranged His universe, but actions inspired by cupidity are constantly disrupting that harmony. To escape the chains of cupidity and take their proper place within the order of the Whole, men need the assistance of Church and Empire.

Dante knew, however, that the Church was far from pure, and the Empire far from powerful. Knowing the deficiencies of these institutions, he wrote The Divine Comedy to assist in emancipating individuals from their enslavement to cupidity. The poem is designed "to remove those living in this life from a state of misery, and bring them to a state of happiness." So Dante himself tells us in his letter to Can Grande della Scala. Dante wrote his poem $_6$ "not for speculation, but with a practical object."[6]

How does one travel from estrangement from the order of the Whole to integration into it, from misery to happiness? The journey has three stages. First comes the recognition that one's will is enslaved to cupidity. This is no abstract affirmation, but an awareness of the full enormity of the nature and consequences of one's captivity. Second, one must purify one's disordered will, replacing cupidity with rightly-ordered love. This is no easy task. While the cultivation of the Aristotelian virtues can assist in this growth, it is not sufficient; man, by his own efforts, cannot save himself. Only with the grace of God can his reorientation be accomplished. Once the will is rightly ordered, one enters the third stage, wherein one's will is perfectly attuned to the will of God. Here, reintegrated into the greater Whole, one finds fulfillment.

For Church and Empire to assist men in their journey, these institutions too must be reordered. Their transformation should follow the same broad course as the reordering of individual life. What is first needed is the recognition of the disorder and

----------

6. Epistolae, Letter X, p. 202.

corruption of a world devoid of the guidance of Church and Empire. Second, man's public institutions (both spiritual and secular) must be brought to fulfill their roles in the divine plan. Finally, once Church and Empire are rightly-ordered, they can exert positive influences on the lives of their subjects, leading them from misery to happiness.[7] Human effort is required to reorder the workings of the public sphere, but such efforts by themselves will not be sufficient. Only when men's actions coincide with the workings of divine Providence will the reordering of public life take place.

Without divine intervention, human felicity is unattainable. Yet Dante claims that the purpose of The Divine Comedy "is to remove those living in this life from a state of misery, and to bring them to a state of happiness." This implies that the poem can achieve something requiring divine aid for its accomplishment. While Dante accurately perceives his exalted greatness as a poet, he does not presume to speak as God. He does, however, claim to speak for God. He speaks as one who has been granted a vision, not only of the road to redemption, but of the Godhead Itself. As Thomas Bergin points out, Dante appears to claim that his work "being a 'true' account, merits the credence if not the veneration accorded to Holy Writ."[8]

Dante's great poem, his "microcosm of the universe," strives mightily to reveal the order of the Whole. Just as fallible men do not directly and immediately discern the fullness of Truth of the Scriptures, so Dante does not expect his readers to immediately grasp his vision of the Whole. He builds into his poem many meanings, meanings which are discernible through the employment of a fourfold method of Scriptural interpretation. This fourfold method, common in Dante's time, interprets the Scriptures as having, in addition to their literal and historical truth, a potential to unfold up to three other true senses, an allegorical sense (figuration), a moral

----------

7. For a similar though not identical treatment of this subject, see Dorothy Sayers, Introductory Papers, p. 112.

8. Dante's Divine Comedy (Englewood Cliffs, N.J.: Prentice-Hall, 1971), p. 90.

sense, and an anagogical (spiritual) sense. Dante himself interprets The Divine Comedy according to this fourfold method in his letter to Can Grande.[9] By deliberately giving his poem manifold meanings, Dante endeavors to share with his readers the richness of his vision of the Whole.

Later generations, not Dante himself, added the adjective Divine to the title of the poem that Dante calls simply his Comedy. But Divine Comedy is the better title. It more exactly expresses the status that Dante attributes to his work. As a kind of divine intervention in the lives of men, the poem can alert men to their predicament and inspire them to strive to bring right order to their wills and their institutions. Unless men make this effort, God's grace goes unsought. The poem is no substitute for the divine response to men's striving. It is, however, a powerful force leading men to undertake that striving. In this way, The Divine Comedy does play its part in leading men from misery to happiness.

The Divine Comedy certainly is the story of Dante's own progression from misery to happiness. Charles Grandgent calls it "a spiritual autobiography in the allegorical shape of a journey through the three realms of the departed, a story of remorse, recognition of sin, reformation, and exaltation of the soul to God."[10] Hell, Purgatory, and Heaven are spiritual states as well as places,[11] and Dante has known them all. He uses his immense poetic abilities to convey this experience to others. The story of his spiritual odyssey is meant to inspire his readers to make their own journeys from misery to happiness.[12]

----------

9. Epistolae, Letter X, p. 199. See also Charles S. Singleton, "Dante's Allegory," Speculum, Vol. XXV (1950), pp. 78-86.

10. Dante Alighieri (New York: Unger, 1966, c. 1916), p. 19.

11. Aldo Bernardo, "Dante's Divine Comedy: The View From God's Eye," in A Dante Symposium, ed. William J. De Sua and Gino Rizzo (Chapel Hill: University of North Carolina Press, 1965), pp. 52ff.

12. Umberto Cosmo, A Handbook to Dante Studies, trans. David Moore (Oxford: Blackwell, 1950), p. 164.

Dante's story is one of redemption. At its beginning he is hopelessly enslaved to cupidity. His
search for God is a tale of spiritual growth culminating in the Beatific Vision. As Bernard Stambler
notes:

> The movement of the Commedia is from the
> condition of being lost in a dark wood to
> the condition of contemplating the Triune
> God and comprehending the meaning of His
> universe. This progress, from nearly total
> ignorance to nearly total knowledge, is
> stepwise, by means of recurrent revelations
> and ever higher and wider syntheses of
> understanding.
>
> These syntheses are perceptions, or
> recognitions, of an identity of things
> that had previously seemed disparate and
> disjunct.[13]

At every stage of his journey, Dante's consciousness
expands. As Stambler brings out, this increased awareness does not deprecate the lesser goods it once
prized. Instead it continuously reevaluates them, now
seeing as manifestations of the divine Goodness what it
had previously taken to be goods in themselves. Thus
Dante can hold a positive valuation of civic life and
the universal Empire while simultaneously recognizing
higher and greater goods than these. Dorothy Sayers
explains the mechanics of Dante's continuing affirmation of the value of earthly goods by noting that his
spiritual path was that of "the Affirmative Way." This
way

> begins with an experience (usually in
> childhood) in which the Divine Glory is
> perceived and apprehended as immanent in
> some created person or thing.... The
> creature is beheld sub specie aeternitatis,
> bathed in and suffused with the light of its
> true and eternal nature--it is seen as God
> sees it.

----------

13. Dante's Other World: the Purgatorio As Guide to the
Divine Comedy (New York: New York University Press,
1957), p. 79.

This experience passes. Later comes a more intellectual and less exalted partial recovery of one's power of apprehension. The final stage is the recovery of the capacity of recognition "but at a much higher and more universal level than before. The glory which was once known only in the beloved creature is diffused upon all creation, and taken up into its Eternal Source".[14] In Dante's case, the original experience was his childhood discernment of the divine glory in Beatrice. The final stage is evident when he returns to Beatrice, that she might help him see the whole universe, including civic life and the Empire, in the light of the Eternal Source.

In the course of arriving at a clearer understanding of the poem, Danteists have developed some special analytical tools. We can use these tools to illuminate the political ideas of the Comedy in the context of the poem as a whole. One such tool requires us to be aware of the perspective from which Dante writes. As Erich Auerbach puts it:

> With the utmost explicitness and consistency, he maintains the attitude of a man who, by special grace, after Aeneas and Paul, has been admitted to see the other world, and has been entrusted with a mission as important as theirs; to reveal to mankind God's eternal order and, accordingly, to teach his fellow men what is wrong in the structure of human life at this special moment of history. The imperial power, ordained to unite and to govern human society, is despised and almost destroyed; the papacy has forgotten its spiritual function; by transgressing its boundaries, by pursuing worldly ambitions and worldly avarice, it has ruined itself and has corrupted the entire human family. Dante goes so far as to describe this disorder as a second fall of man.[15]

----------

14. Sayers, Introductory Papers, pp. 123-124.

15. "Dante's Address to the Reader," in American Critical Essays on the Divine Comedy, ed. Robert J. Clements (New York: New York University Press, 1967), p. 44.

This is the position of Dante the author or narrator, and it is often significantly different from the thinking of Dante the protagonist, the pilgrim who undertakes the journey from dark wood to highest Heaven. Thus there are two Dantes in The Divine Comedy; one, the author, narrates the story and throws out occasional words of warning or encouragement to the reader. This Dante-Author looks down from his lofty perch at the actions of the other Dante, Dante-Pilgrim, as the latter makes his way imperfectly along his course. This distinction is made by virtually all modern commentators on Dante's poem. Its consequences are important. We cannot treat the speeches of Dante the Pilgrim as if they were the mature thinking of Dante-Author. This they are not. They are the ideas of one whose consciousness is still restricted. Similar caution must be exercised in evaluating the words of other characters in the poem. They too frequently imperfectly understand the things of which they speak. While their ideas may not on this account be dismissed, neither can they be entirely taken as Dante's own. "If we want to know what the spiritual sense of the whole work is," says Dorothy Sayers, "we must look, first, foremost and all the time, at the movement of the story as a whole--not, primarily, to obiter dicta thrown out by the characters, who may be speaking in character."[16]

A second useful tool for understanding the poem is to recognize that it has multiple strands of meaning. For our purposes the most significant of these meanings are moral and political. The moral meaning of the poem deals with individuals. Here and now in this world individuals must live with the consequences of the choices they make. The Inferno shows the spiritual condition of those whose choices are rooted in their enslavement to cupidity. The Purgatorio depicts the state of penitent souls striving to put their loves in order. The Paradiso reveals the bliss of purified souls enjoying both temporal happiness and spiritual fulfillment in the awareness of God's immediate presence.

The Comedy's political meaning concerns public life. The Inferno reflects a disordered world. The Purgatorio presents the picture of society in the

----------

16. Introductory Papers, p. 103.

process of reestablishing right order. The _Paradiso_
shows the harmonious functioning of a rightly-ordered
universal monarchy.[17] We can better grasp the political content of _The Divine Comedy_ if we keep in mind
this overall structure. The poem's political meaning
runs parallel to its simpler and more obvious moral
meaning. Sometimes the two strands of meaning inter-
twine. Consequently, we will more easily understand
the political teaching of the poem if we look first at
its moral and then at its political meaning. This is
the procedure we shall follow in considering the
_Inferno_, the _Purgatorio_, and the _Paradiso_.

----------

17. See Sayers, _Introductory Papers_, p. 112.

# Chapter 3

## THE INFERNO

Book One of the Comedy, the Inferno, is literally a description of Dante-Pilgrim's journey through Hell. Hell is filled with men and women who died unrepentant sinners. Assigned to different parts of Hell according to the nature of their sin, they suffer torments appropriate to their wrongdoing.

On a deeper level, as we know from Dante's letter to Can Grande, the Comedy deals with the living. The Inferno depicts living individuals and societies moved by disordered love: cupidity. Cupidity is the willing embrace of some lesser good as an end in itself, to the exclusion of the greater good of God. Living sinners eagerly seek the lesser goods that do not satisfy. Like the unrepentant dead of the Inferno, who are eager to cross the river Acheron into Hell, living sinners choose to be something other than what God wills them to be. In this they resemble Satan, Hell's first inhabitant. "It is" says Dorothy Sayers "the deliberate choosing to remain in illusion and to see God and the universe as hostile to one's ego that is the very essence of Hell."[1] God's will is rejected in favor of a foredoomed attempt to find fulfillment in the vain flounderings of one's own isolated willfulness.[2] Misery, symbolized by the torments of Hell, is the consequence of such mistaken choices.

People mischoose out of ignorance. Lack of true discernment has led Hell's inhabitants to choose as they have. Dante's informant on this matter is Virgil, who, having made a previous journey through Hell, is knowledgeable about its inhabitants. They are, he

----------

1. Introductory Papers, p. 66.

2. Matheson, Character and Citizenship in Dante," p. 866.

27

says, "the woeful people who have lost the good of the intellect."[3] For Dante, the intellect involves more than the calculating capacity; it also includes man's powers of intuition and imagination.[4] In it is rooted the faculty of judgment. The good of the intellect embraces the ability to judge rightly amongst the goods of this life, so that one can choose goods that lead to fulfillment in God rather than goods that exalt the individual will in opposition to the will of God. Those who have lost the good of the intellect lack the discernment to choose rightly; their choices lead to misery rather than happiness.

The discernible agonies of Hell's inhabitants are the outward depiction of the interior sufferings of living men and women who choose undiscerningly. Sin carries its own punishment, in this world as in the next. Dante's picture of Hell says much about what life is like for those who have lost the light of the intellect. First, Hell is underground. It is cut off from the light of the sun, symbolizing the darkness of the soul which has cut itself off from the light of God. Second, Hell is an inverted cone. The circumference of its base intersects the earth's surface, and its apex is the earth's center. Bernard Stambler perceptively sees the significance of this shape:

> The spread-outness of the opening of the
> cone portrays a deceptively wide area of
> choice: it is wide only in its provision of
> a multitude of wrong choices. As one
> descends inside the cone of the Inferno [one
> experiences] the unremitting constric-
> tiveness of the place....[5]

----------

3. _Inferno_, Canto III, 17-18. All quotations in English from _The Divine Comedy_ are reprinted by permittion of the Bodley Head Ltd. from _The Divine Comedy of Dante Alighieri_ translated by John D. Sinclair, (New York: Oxford University Press, 1965, c. 1939-1945.) 3 vols.

4. Dorothy Sayers, _Further Papers on Dante_ (New York: Harper, 1957), p. 43.

5. _Dante' Other World_, p. 86.

For persons living in this world, sin is bondage. When the power of judgment is obscured, when appetite rules in its place, man's freedom of choice is lost.[6] The geography of Hell expresses this truth. Not only is it an inverted cone, but each infernal inhabitant is strictly confined to a single part of Hell. As the shades (souls of the dead) are confined to their particular corner of the underworld, so are living sinners bound by their ruling loves. Furthermore, in Dante's Hell the force of gravity increases as one descends toward the earth's center. The deeper the living sink in sin, the more burdensome, confining and unfree are their lives.

On the moral level, the Inferno shows the nature of cupidity, of disordered love. Politically it reveals the effects of disordered love on social and political life. Unrestrained cupidity characterizes political life on earth almost as much as it characterizes life in Hell. This parallel should not surprise us. Both Hell and earth lack a politically powerful Empire and a spiritually pure Church to curb man's cupidity and direct him towards higher goods. Politically, the Inferno addresses the disordered political life of Europe, just as morally it portrays the disordered loves of living individuals.

Canto I sets the stage for Dante's journey. Dante tells how in mid-life he discovers himself in a dark wood, having lost the straight way. Leaving the wood, he arrives at the foot of a beautiful hill behind which the sun is rising. Limping somewhat on his left foot, he attempts to climb this delectable mountain. His progress is impeded by a swift leopard, but he remains hopeful of making the ascent. A fierce lion takes the place of the leopard and in turn is replaced by a she-wolf "which appeared in its leanness to be charged with all cravings."[7] Disheartened by the terrible she-wolf he retreats toward the dark wood. Unexpectedly he finds Virgil there, whom he acknowledges as "my master and my author."[8] The greedy she-wolf lets no man make the straight ascent up the mountain, Virgil tells him.

----------

6. A. F. G. Howell, Dante: His Life and Work (London: Jack, 1912), p. 75.

7. Inferno I, 49-50.

8. Inferno I, 85.

The day shall come, however, when the Veltro, the hound, shall drive her back to Hell. For the present, Dante's best hope is to accept Virgil as guide for a journey through Hell and Purgatory. At the journey's end Virgil promises to deliver Dante into the hands of someone more qualified (Beatrice), who will conduct him through Heaven. Dante agrees and they set out together.

On the moral level this canto states what any man must do to commence the journey from misery to happiness. The first step occurs when one recognizes the seriousness of one's plight, symbolized by Dante-Pilgrim's coming to himself in the dark wood where the straight way is lost. The tracklessness of the wood symbolizes a life spent in pursuit of lesser goods to the exclusion of the supreme good of God. The poem is set at Easter of 1300, Dante's thirty-fifth year, a time when he was intensely absorbed in the political life of Florence, perhaps so absorbed that his previous heavenward aspiration, inspired by Beatrice and recorded in the Vita Nuova, was forgotten. The darkness of the wood indicates the absence of the light of God. This is a common human situation. The goods of earthly existence are absorbing, and one can pursue them fixedly, quite unconscious of one's spiritual blindness. But even at the outset of the poem Dante-Pilgrim has emerged from this condition. He has come to himself and has reached the edge of the wood, where the light of God (the sun) is rising so that its rays bathe the hill.

Dante's seeing the dawning sun represents his intellect's dawning cognition of life's true good, God. This is an essential step in the journey from misery to felicity. But by itself it is not enough. Not only must the true Good be perceived, but the will must be purged of those appetites which deflect the soul from pursuit of that Good. This purgation of the will is symbolized by the ascent of "the delectable mountain [Purgatory] which is the beginning and cause of all happiness."[9] The will must be purged, the delectable mountain must be climbed, which Dante-Pilgrim attempts to do, albeit in a limping, irresolute fashion. But he fails. He is driven back and disheartened by the terrifying she-wolf, the symbol of cupidity. Man's unaided attempts to purify himself and

----------

9. Inferno I, 77-78.

30

ascend to God are thwarted by the surprising intensity, the terrifying intensity, of his own cupidity.[10] It is at this stage that Virgil appears. Virgil explains that the she-wolf prevents not only Dante but all men from directly ascending the hill. The direct route up the delectable mountain being cut off, Dante must progress indirectly, journeying through the bowels of Hell before attempting the mountain of Purgatory. The pilgrim soul must undertake a direct exploration of the nature and consequences of its cupidity. Only then can it truly and categorically repent its sinfulness and begin the purgation of its disordered loves. In his first-hand exploration of the consequences of disordered love, Dante-Pilgrim takes Virgil for his guide. Ancient knowledge and wisdom, symbolized by Virgil, can help bring the Christian pilgrim to his goal. The moral virtues of Aristotelian philosophy can help guide the Christian soul on the difficult interior journey that leads to purgation and ultimately to happiness.

The political strand of meaning of this canto runs parallel with and strengthens the moral strand. The dark and trackless wood is the world, abandoned to disorder by its rulers (Emperor and Pope) who are themselves enslaved by cupidity. The leopard, lion and she-wolf are vices, which in the absence of a strong Emperor to restrain them, dominate the world of living men.[11] Dominated by bad men, public life no longer performs the important function of nurturing the natural human virtues which help man climb the delectable mountain. Many people are consequently denied the enjoyment of the natural felicity that comes with the performance of virtuous action. As Dante in due course makes clear, people are thereby denied also the opportunity to rise from the natural felicity of virtuous action to the subsequent supernatural felicity of spiritual illumination, symbolized by the sun's rising behind the mountain. But, Virgil tells Dante, it will not always be so. The hound (Veltro) will come and drive the she-wolf back to Hell. This prophecy

----------

10. See Aldo Bernardo, "The Three Beasts and Perspective in the Divine Comedy," PMLA, LXXVII (1963), 17, and Lawrence Baldassaro, "Dante the Pilgrim: Everyman as Sinner," in Dante Studies, XCII (1974), 65.

11. On this point see Howell, Dante, pp. 67-69.

indicates a coming restoration of public order which will put cupidity to flight.[12] Then man's participation in a rightly-ordered political community, one which nourishes human virtue, will facilitate his ascending the mountain of God. But for the present, while his temporal and spiritual rulers are gripped by cupidity, man must make the internal pilgrimage of the individual soul largely unaided by public authority.[13]

Virgil foretells the coming of the Veltro. Does Dante-Author subscribe to this prophecy? To answer this question we need to consider both Virgil's credibility as a spokesman for Dante and his significance in the poem. Virgil is a leading character in The Divine Comedy. He does not stand for any single thing, but for many things. Most commonly he is said to represent reason in the Comedy, and this he certainly does. Virgil also represents poetry. He stands as well for ancient philosophy, particularly the Aristotelian moral philosophy whose praises Dante sang in the Banquet. On the political level Virgil symbolizes Rome and the universal Roman Empire. He represents a whole cluster of things, all of which have significant common features. All reached a high level of development in the ancient world. All are achieved through the employment of man's natural capacities, but without the benefit of divine revelation. All point beyond themselves to something greater, a spiritual reality that is very much evident in Dante's poem. For Dante, philosophy reached its high point in the work of Aristotle, an ancient Greek. Aristotle saw philosophy, the supreme exercise of man's reason, as a divine activity, something above the purely human level. Medieval civilization, however, saw philosophy not as a divine activity, but as the handmaiden of theology. Poetry reached its zenith in the work of Virgil, who Dante calls "my master and my author", yet Virgil's poetry points beyond itself as well. The medievals saw Virgil as not simply the celebrator of Rome, her history, and her worldwide empire, but as one who, in his Fourth Eclogue, dimly foretold the coming of Christ. The Roman Empire represented for Dante the height of human political achievement, and at the same time Dante believed that the Roman Empire was the necessary precondition for Christ's coming into the world to perform his

----------

12. D'Entrèves, Dante as a Political Thinker, p. 5.

13. Howell, Dante, p. 69.

32

redemptive task. Virgil thus sums up for Dante all that was best in the classical world: ancient philosophy, ancient poetry, ancient political order. All these things point beyond themselves, beyond the rational, the natural, and the secular to the spiritual, the supernatural, the eternal. In the dramatic action of the poem, Virgil, noble himself within his own limits, leads beyond these limits to one who is able to transport Dante to Heaven: Beatrice.[14] Virgil is at once the personification of what can be achieved by purely human, natural means, and the demonstration that these achievements are not sufficient, they must be transcended.

In evaluating Virgil's words, we need to be aware of both his strengths and his shortcomings. Canto II reveals both. It tells how Mary, the Empress of Heaven, in her grace sent Saint Lucy to Beatrice, who in turn sent Virgil to the aid of Dante-Pilgrim. That Virgil should be chosen for such a mission indicates his worth. His shortcoming is revealed by the journey Beatrice has to undertake to find him. Unlike Beatrice, Lucy and Mary, all of whom dwell in the court of God, Virgil is in Hell. These facts show that Virgil, the symbol of human reason and human achievement, is both a worthy and an inadequate guide in life. His knowledge is true knowledge, but it is not the whole truth. It lacks something crucial, knowledge of life's spiritual, supernatural, eternal dimension. Yet despite its deficiency Virgil's knowledge is not to be dismissed. Dante greatly admired the accomplishments of ancient culture, represented in the poem by Virgil. Indeed, Dante sees this secular culture as God's means of guiding man in temporal affairs.[15] Virgil's knowledge is, within its limits, true knowledge.

As a spokesman for the views of Dante-Author, Virgil's words can be trusted when they deal with natural, human, secular matters. In this sphere Virgil's

----------

14. See Rocco Montano, "Dante and Virgil," Yale Review, LX (1971), 554-555; Whitfield, Dante and Virgil, pp. 72-73; Sayers, Further Papers, p. 56.

15. See Jennifer Petrie, "Dante's Virgil: Purgatorio XXX," in David Nolan, ed., Dante Soundings, (Dublin: Irish Academic Press, 1981), pp. 132-133.

knowledge is valid. The speeches in which Virgil acknowledges the limits of purely human knowledge should
also be understood as statements of the views of
Dante-Author. One of Virgil's primary functions in the
Comedy is to point beyond the natural to the supernatural; in this he clearly speaks for Dante-Author.
Finally, since Virgil, like the other citizens of Hell,
has the capacity to know in advance forthcoming earthly
events, his prophecies, such as the one that the
she-wolf will some day be banished by the Veltro, are
to be taken seriously. We can thus conclude that
Dante-Author genuinely believed in the coming of a
restored public order as symbolized by the Veltro's
driving away the she-wolf.

    Virgil is Dante's immediate guide, but it is
Beatrice who has sent Virgil to Dante. Just as Virgil
is himself, the Roman poet, and also, symbolically,
much more, so Beatrice is herself, the real Beatrice
whom Dante loved and who was for him a revelation of
the divine glory, and she is also a symbol. Beatrice
symbolizes revelation, spiritual illumination, grace,
theology, salvation, and even Christ.[16] If Virgil's
speeches must be weighed before being accepted as the
views of Dante-Author, no such caution needs to be
taken in the case of Beatrice. Her words are meant
to be revealed truth, and represent Dante's mature
opinion.

    Virgil acts at Beatrice's command. This relation-
ship is vitally important. Human secular achievement
as represented in the best of ancient civilization
(Virgil) cannot by itself bring fallen man to
felicity. Only when prompted by spiritual grace
(Beatrice) can it familiarize man with the nature of
his disordered love and help him purge himself of his
cupidity. Secular and spiritual advancement go hand in
hand for Dante. Without divine inspiration, secular
guides lead at best to Virgil's home in Limbo, and not
to earthly or heavenly felicity.[17]

----------

16. See Bernardo, "View From God's Eye," p. 49; Sayers,
Introductory Papers, pp. xv, 8, 190; Charles S.
Singleton, Dante Studies II: Journey to Beatrice,
(Cambridge: Harvard University Press, 1958),
pp. 43, 89.

17. Sayers, Further Papers, pp. 45-47, 113.
                        34

The third major character in Canto II who commands our attention is Dante-Pilgrim. Virgil tells the story of his commissioning by Beatrice to dispel Dante's doubts at undertaking this perilous journey through the underworld. Now that the time has come to set out, Dante-Pilgrim is afraid. After all, who is he to journey where previously only men of the stature of Aeneas and St. Paul have trod? Such pusillanimity reminds us that Dante-Pilgrim himself is weak, and not a source to be trusted uncritically. We cannot necessarily accept the words of Dante-Pilgrim as reliable statements of the ideas of Dante-Author.

As Canto III begins, Virgil and Dante pass through the gate of Hell, whose inscription ends with the famous words "ABANDON EVERY HOPE, YE THAT ENTER."[18] Hell is dark, as cut off from the light of the sun as sinful men are cut off from the light of God. Hell is dismal, as we would expect of a world cut off from the light of its two proper luminaries, a faithful Church and an effective Empire.[19] Just inside Hell's gate Dante encounters the neutrals, those who did nothing, risked nothing, either for evil or for good, and consequently won neither disgrace nor praise. They are miserable, says Virgil (and in Hell, where he has travelled before, Virgil is a reliable commentator). They cannot hope for death, neither can they hope for remembrance on earth. Pity and justice despise them.[20]

The desire of earthly remembrance is something the neutrals share with many (though not all) of Hell's subjects. In the Inferno, when Dante-Pilgrim meets a shade whose story he wishes to know, he promises to add to its earthly fame.[21] This inducement is largely successful. But the neutrals have no fame and Virgil discourages Dante-Pilgrim from even speaking to them.

The desire for fame is shared even by Virgil. So Beatrice thinks at least, for when she wishes to send him to Dante's aid she begins her address: "O Courteous

----------

18. Inferno III, 9.

19. See Purgatorio XVI, 106-108.

20. Inferno III, 46-49.

21. Matheson, "Character and Citizenship," p. 873.

Mantuan soul, whose fame still endures in the world and shall endure as long as the world lasts."[22] She would hardly entreat him thus unless she thought that fame appealed to him. But unlike Dante-Pilgrim's promises of lasting remembrance to those he meets in Hell, Beatrice promises Virgil another, and much greater kind of fame. She closes her request of him with the words "when I am before my Lord I will often speak to Him in praise of thee."[23] She offers not remembrance in the minds of men but praise in the court of God.

In promising to preserve for future generations the renown of great men, Dante-Pilgrim undertakes no more than to fulfill one of the most ancient political functions of a poet. George F. Jones, for example, notes that "German poets had long looked upon themselves as the proprietors and propagators of their lieges' honor and fame."[24] Fame appeals to public men, and for that fame to endure, it needs to be recorded and transmitted to future generations. Fame is an important human value, one which politicians and poets both esteem. That fame should strongly appeal to the damned says much about Dante-Author's own views. Dante was not one to disparage poets, nor to belittle politics. Yet preserving the fame of earthly men is clearly in itself of no great value. Both fame and its preservation are compatible with damnation, with a life lived in enslavement to cupidity and devoid of the light of God. In the eternal scale of things, earthly fame has no weight.

The fame that Beatrice offers Virgil, however, is of a different quality. Praise before God, by one of Heaven's citizens, is no mean good. If Virgil cannot join the heavenly court in person, he can at least be there in the words of Beatrice. Symbolically, this indicates that while the pre-Christian civilization of Virgil cannot by itself bring man to felicity, its worth is considerable when supplemented by spiritual

----------

22. Inferno II, 58-60.

23. Inferno II, 73-74.

24. Honor in German Literature (Chapel Hill: University of North Carolina Press, 1959), p. 81. On the political function of the poet in antiquity, see Hannah Arendt, The Human Condition (Chicago: University of Chicago Press, 1958), p. 197.

grace (Beatrice). Dante is no Manichean preaching the evil of the material world. He genuinely valued the accomplishments of ancient civilization. It is Virgil, after all, who is Dante-Pilgrim's guide and companion on his journey to Beatrice. Accordingly, Virgil and all that he symbolizes are in the Divine Light, if only at second hand.

This is the situation Dante-Pilgrim finds when he visits Virgil's home in Limbo in Canto IV. In the darkness of Hell a pool of light illumines the dwelling of the noblest of the ancient pagans. The achievements of antiquity's greatest poets, philosophers and public men have won them a measure of approval in Heaven. "Their honorable fame," Virgil tells Dante, "which resounds in thy life above, gains favor in Heaven which thus advances them."[25]

The virtuous heathens live, significantly, in a castle, surrounded by seven walls and by a stream. While in Hell these defenses are unnecessary, in life they are needed. Human virtue has an implacable foe, cupidity. On the moral or individual level the seven hills symbolize the seven virtues (four moral and three intellectual) of classical ethics. On the political level the seven walls and the stream symbolize imperial Rome, surrounded by her seven fortified hills and the river Tiber.[26] As the virtues subdue cupidity in the individual and contribute to the growth of rightly-ordered love in his soul, so Rome subdued and brought order to the ancient world.

Limbo's virtuous heathens have developed man's natural powers in isolation from his spiritual capacities. Kenelm Foster writes that Dante's Limbo reflects:

> the emergence in the European mind at that time of an idea of human perfectibility to be realized before death and within the limits of human nature; this being distinguished, with quite new precision,

----------

25. Inferno IV, 76-78.

26. Jefferson B. Fletcher, "Dante's School of the Eagle," Romanic Review, XXII (1931), 192-193.

37

from the 'new man' of Christian teaching,
from our nature as transformed by divine
grace.[27]

The achievements of Dante's virtuous heathens are re-
warded; they live in light, but in a light enclosed by
darkness. In this they differ from the purified
Christian souls who experience the fulfillment of their
natural powers in the Garden of Eden upon the summit of
Mount Purgatory. Unlike Limbo, Eden is lit by the sun,
symbolic of God. Here men of faith exercise their
natural capacities perfectly, in accord with the will
of their Creator. By contrast, the accomplishments of
Limbo's virtuous heathens, while truly great, are insufficient.[28] For all their public and private virtues, they lacked the faith necessary to worship God
aright[29] and thus gain entrance to Purgatory. "Faith
is imagination actualized by the will" Dorothy Sayers
writes; "what was lacking to Virgil's faith was
precisely the imagination. To the great heathen Dante
allotted just that beatitude which they were able to
imagine for themselves."[30]

Virgil's failing is the converse of that of Dante-
Pilgrim.[31] Dante's will, not his imagination, is what is
lacking. On emerging from the dark wood, he saw not
only the delectable mountain but the sun [God] rising
above it. What defeated Dante was the she-wolf,
cupidity so powerful as to overpower the will despite
the imagination's vision. Virgil is thus a fit teacher
and companion for Dante. Virgil has mastered precisely
what Dante has yet to master, the disciplining of the
will. By his example, by his words of encouragement,
by his shaming of Dante, he can help Dante keep
cupidity in check, just as the Empire can help keep

----------

27. "The Two Dantes: III," in The Two Dantes and Other
Studies, (Berkeley: University of California Press,
1978), p. 220.

28. Sinclair, Inferno, pp. 69-70.

29. Inferno IV, 34-38.

30. Further Papers, p. 32.

31. See John Freccero, "Dante's Firm Foot and the
Journey Without a Guide," Harvard Theological Review,
LII (1959), 245-281.

man's cupidity in check by its enforcement of just laws. By the end of the _Inferno_ Dante has come far in disciplining his will, for the irresolute, pusillanimous, easily discouraged figure of the _Inferno_'s early cantos could never have made the journey through Hell successfully without disciplining his will. But there is a great difference between disciplining the will, holding cupidity in check, which Virgil and the virtuous pagans did well, and transforming cupidiity into a qualitatively different phenomenon, rightly-ordered love. This demands true repentance, a steadfast will to transform, and not merely restrain, one's appetites. Such repentance is inspired by the imagination's recognition of the beauty of a soul in harmony with God and the ugliness of a life that puts God second to the enjoyment of lesser things. By the time Dante-Pilgrim emerges from Hell, he possesses the requisite will, as well as the necessary imagination. Purgatory will be open to him. But Virgil, lacking imagination, lacked faith. He lacked an essential prerequisite of the purgative process. Limbo therefore is his home.

In Cantos four through eight, Dante sees the punishments experienced by sinners who, lacking self-control, have become enslaved by sexual love, gluttony, avarice, prodigality or anger. Thereupon Dante and Virgil approach the City of Dis. Hell's city is everything that a body politic should not be. Injustice rather than justice characterizes its citizens, for they give neither God, their neighbors, nor right action their due. The disordered wills of these shades prevent them from cooperating with one another in any common undertaking. Isolated, confused, mutually antagonistic, the inhabitants of Dis lead a life of strife and sorrow, a life devoid of hope or harmony.[32]

Fallen angels close the gates of Dis against Virgil and Dante; Virgil's words fail to gain them entrance. The earthly Empire, acting with merely natural virtue, cannot by itself prevail against the disorder of a city in rebellion against God, Satan's city, which boasts fallen angels as its guardians. Divine intervention is needed, and is received with the

----------

32. Eric Auerbach, _Dante, Poet of the Secular World_, trans. Ralph Manheim (Chicago: University of Chicago Press, 1961, c. 1929), pp. 130-131.

coming of an angel who opens the gate to Virgil and Dante-Pilgrim. Only with spiritual aid can earthly virtue and right order triumph over disorder.

The first circle within the walls of Dis holds the heretics. For Dante-Author, heresy evidently involves more than erroneous belief in matters of Christian faith. Epicurus, a pagan, is there, and with him many nominally Christian shades who in life have denied the immortality of the soul and lived only for earthly happiness. In particular some Ghibellines, partisans of the Emperor's party in Italian politics, are found here, among them the Emperor Frederick II, "the Cardinal" (Cardinal Ottaviano degli Ubaldini), and, most notably, Farinata degli Uberti. In lumping these shades together, Dante-Author draws our attention to the divisive nature of heresy, its failure to appreciate the wholeness, the unity of God's creation. Heresy involves identification with a part, be it one's body, one's political faction, or even one's country, to the exclusion of the greater Whole. According to Irma Brandeis "this failure occurs when the ego clings to some fraction or splinter of the whole, which it itself has nurtured."[33] Epicurus clings to the body and denies the soul, and all those who follow his way find themselves cut off from the entire spiritual dimension of God's universe. On the political level, both Church and Empire have had their unity sundered by sects and factions that have clung obstinately to their own particularity.

Dante-Author is especially concerned to denounce factionalism in earthly politics. Farinata may be in this circle in part because of his Epicureanism, but his conversation with Dante focuses on political matters. In Hell as on earth, Farinata classifies people as friend or foe, Ghibelline or Guelf. He immediately recognizes Dante (a Guelf in 1300, the time in which the poem is set) as an enemy. He takes no notice whatsoever of the Guelf Cavalcante de' Cavalcanti, who shares his tomb with him, despite having married his daughter to Cavalcanti's son in an unsuccessful attempt to reconcile Florentine Guelfs and Ghibellines. Brandeis writes: "the image of Farinata and Cavalcanti, shut eternally in a single tomb,

----------

33. The Ladder of Vision: A Study of Dante's Comedy (Garden City, N.Y.: Doubleday, 1961), p. 42.

suffering the same flames, yet unaware of one another, stands for the whole concept of divisiveness."[34] The narrowness of vision that Farinata and Cavalcanti display in Hell is the same narrowness of vision that shatters the peace and unity of earthly civilization, and creates a Hell on earth. It is significant that Dante chooses to exemplify the vice of factionalism in a Ghibelline. It is the blindness to the Whole that factionalism encourages that Dante deplores, and he deplores this blindness as much in the nominal partisans of the universal Empire as in the Empire's opponents.

Farinata, however, is an attractive character. Proud, uncomplaining, still convinced of the merit of his life's actions, he is a figure that Dante-Pilgrim treats with respect. On earth he was a great man, and if he was (and is) bitterly partisan, he was also a great patriot. He stood alone in defense of Florence when the Italian Ghibellines, victorious in the battle of Montaperti in 1260, proposed her destruction. He succeeded in defeating that project. Like many characters in the _Inferno_, Farinata is appealing. Such figures display the attractive character of being bound up in the love of secondary goods. Limited earthly goods are attractive. If they were not, no one would choose them. But great deeds and great patriotism cannot redeem one whose vision and whose will are forever directed only to a part and never to the Whole.

We can draw from this encounter two conclusions. One is that Dante-Author firmly rejects factionalism, even a factionalism that takes the form of devotion to the Imperial cause. The other is his rejection of Epicureanism, the denial of the immortality of the soul that was entertained by some Ghibellines. The (reputed) words of Ottaviano degli Ubaldini, "the Cardinal", whom Dante-Pilgrim here recognizes, exemplify both sins: "If there is a soul, I have lost mine a thousand times for the Ghibellines."[35] Dante wanted a universal Empire that would be receptive to the spiritual teaching of the Church, an Empire whose officials would be sincere Christians.

----------

34. _Ladder_, p. 46.

35. Sinclair, _Inferno_, p. 139, note 10.

41

In Canto XII Dante and Virgil come to the pond of
boiling blood, Phlegethon. Those who have done violence to others must endure its heat and stench. The
more serious their crime, the deeper they are plunged
into the seething blood. Political violence is the
worst. Violent tyrants are immersed in boiling blood
up to their foreheads. Tyranny here brings no glory,
even for Alexander the Great. "Phlegethon", Sinclair
declares, "is Dante's challenge to military adventure
and public violence, with all their glory and gain;
here they share the penalty of footpads and cut
throats."[36]

In Canto XIII Dante and Virgil come to the wood of
the suicides, where they meet Piero della Vigne,
onetime chancellor to the Emperor Frederick II. After
a lifetime of honored and faithful service, he was
(falsely, he claims) accused of treason. Blinded and
imprisoned, he committed suicide.[37] His story shows
how fortune can lift one to high office and, despite
faultless conduct, dash one down again. Piero is
induced to talk by the promise that his fame on earth
will be revived. It was the disgrace, the scorn of his
earthly fellows, that induced him to kill himself.
Valuing worldly honor and position, he lacked the
internal resources to withstand public humiliation.
Again Dante tells us that the love of earthly fame, so
attractive to public men, is no solid foundation for
living life. To love fame above all is a form of
cupidity, a love for a good lesser than the highest
good, God. It leads to misery, not happiness.

Cantos XV and XVI deal with those who have been
violent against nature. The traditional interpretation
of the poem identifies the shades in this circle as
sodomites.[38] In a number of works Richard Kay argues
that the violent against nature are rather secular
leaders who have failed to discharge faithfully their

----------

36. Sinclair, Inferno, pp. 164-165.

37. See Sinclair, Inferno, p. 174, note 4.

38. See Sinclair, Inferno, p. 193.

responsibilities to direct mankind toward earthly happiness in accord with nature.[39] Two sorts of secular leaders are required to direct mankind, political authorities to uphold the law of the Empire, and intellectuals to instruct men in the truths of natural reason. Two troops of shades are found in this circle. One is composed of renegade politicians who have rebelled against the natural order of the Empire. Deceiving intellectuals, men who have misused their powers of reason, perversely advocating and justifying the defiance of the renegade politicians, make up the other. The chief characters in these cantos, all Florentines, are "intellectuals and political leaders who have established [in Florence] an autarchic civil society that was contrary to nature."[40] Kay argues that "because of their reverence for Dante, his commentators have not considered the possibility that the charge of sodomy was in fact so outrageously false that the poet insinuated it with deliberate intent to shock his readers" into realizing "that the poet's conception of unnatural vice was something more subtle than sodomy".[41] This may indeed be so; certainly Kay's discernment of a more subtle political meaning for these cantos is persuasive. But his case does not depend on acquitting the characters of these cantos of the charge of sodomy. The political meaning he reveals would exist even if the characters of these cantos were sodomites. Thus the meaning Kay discerns in these cantos may be compatible with the older interpretation. Both meanings could have been intended by Dante, whose poem often proceeds simultaneously on the moral or individual level and on the political level. In accepting Kay's interpretation as a valid statement of the political meaning of these cantos, we must note its consequences. Dante-Author is reaffirming both the value of natural reason for discerning the truths of life that can direct mankind toward temporal happiness, and the value of the Empire for upholding the law that

----------

39. "The Sin of Brunetto Latini," Medieval Studies, XXXI (1969), 262-286; "Dante's Unnatural Lawyer: Francesco d'Accorso in Inferno XV", in Studia Gratiana, XV (1972), 147-200; Dante's Swift and Strong: Essays on Inferno XV (Lawrence, Kansas: Regents Press of Kansas, 1978).

40. Dante's Swift and Strong, p. 25.

41. Dante's Swift and Strong, p. 7.

orders men's lives in accordance with these truths. Even though Dante holds that grace must supplement nature for man to find fulfillment, he has a distinctly positive valuation of philosophy and the Empire, and a distinctly negative valuation of those who would subvert them.

Dante-Author's condemnation of perverse secular leaders is followed by his denunciation of corrupt church leaders, men who have used their office not to advance man's spiritual well-being, but to indulge their own greed for wealth. Having betrayed their spiritual calling for worldly gain, they are condemned to Hell. Canto XIX depicts the abode of the simonists, those who, "rapacious, prostitute for gold and silver the things of God which should be brides of righteousness."[42] Three popes of Dante's time qualify for this location. Herbert W. Smith captures much of the import of this canto when he writes "Dante is ever conscious that alongside the conquest of the world by Christianity has come the conquest of the Church by the world."[43]

The political meaning of this canto is important. In Dante's thinking the Church is one of mankind's two great public institutions. Its obsessive greed is one of the fundamental wrongs in the world. The worldliness of the popes was the cause of their vigorous immersion in affairs that were properly the concern of the Empire. Instead of shedding spiritual light on the Empire, they sought temporal power for themselves, thereby doubly weakening the Empire. Dante-Author heightens the political import of this canto when in lines 115-117 he rues the Donation of Constantine. This alleged donation by the Emperor Constantine of temporal authority to the Church increased the worldliness of the Church and diminished the authority of the Empire. These sharp words are spoken by Dante-Pilgrim, who Virgil thereupon takes in his arms. This embrace by Virgil, a reliable spokesman for Dante-Author on political matters, clearly indicates that these sentiments are Dante-Author's own.[44] The simony of leading

----------

42. Inferno XIX, 2-4.

43. The Greatness of Dante Alighieri (Bath: Bath University Press, 1974), p. 99.

44. See Sinclair Inferno, pp. 245-246.

44

churchmen is a source of political as well as spiritual
disorder.

Virgil and Dante next meet the political equi-
valent of the simonists, the barrators. These earthly
officeholders accepted bribes. Perverting justice,
betraying the interests of their fellow citizens, they
truly belong in the City of Dis. Dante-Author mocks
their love of gold. The barrators simmer in a lake of
boiling pitch; the luster of gold has been exchanged
for the blackness of tar. Two entire cantos are
devoted to political corruption. By their end there is
no mistaking the pettiness, the meanness of spirit of
those who stoop to it. Such rascality is utterly
devoid of nobility and attractiveness.

Cantos XXVI and XXVII bring Dante-Pilgrim to the
edge of a ditch wherein he finds the shades of two
noted men of action, one ancient, the other contemporary. Ulysses, the ancient, is Homer's character and
more. He is still the man who persuaded Achilles to go
to his death in the war against Troy, and who tricked
the Trojans with the device of the wooden horse. But
according to Dante, he is also a man who, in his old
age, once more persuaded his companions to leave home,
this time to sail boldly out into the unknown watery
hemisphere. There they sighted the mountain of Purgatory, from whence a storm arose to sink their ship
and bring their adventure to a fatal end. The other
shade, Guido da Montefeltro, was a crafty Ghibelline
military leader who repented his ways and turned
Franciscan monk. Pope Boniface VIII, with the promise
of absolution for the sin Guido would incur, ordered
Guido to employ once again his old craft. Guido
counselled Boniface that in his war with the Colonna
family "large promise with scant observance will make
thee truimph,"[45] which indeed it did.

Guido and Ulysses have much in common. Both are
skilled in action, and love to exercise their talents.
Both men settled down in their later years after an
adventurous early life, but both were tempted to make
one last excursion into the life of action, which
turned out to be their downfall. James Truscott writes
that "the single, irrestible trait in both men's

----------

45. Inferno XXVII, 110-111.

characters is a particular kind of _hubris_ which[46]
ineluctably impels them to just one more attempt."
Ulysses, moved by a "passion...to gain experience of
the world and of the vices and worth of men"[47] exulted
in the power of human daring. His eloquent address to
his companions on their sailing into the unknown watery
hemisphere infected them with his fatal enthusiasm.

> "O brothers...who through a hundred thousand
> perils have reached the west, to this so
> brief vigil of the senses that remains to us
> choose not to deny experience, in the sun's
> track, of the unpeopled world. Take thought
> of the seed from which you spring. You were
> not born to live as brutes, but to follow
> virtue and knowledge".[48]

Guido, a Christian and a monk, well knows the need to
put his deceitful past behind him. But when sought out
by Boniface and offered absolution in advance for the
sin he will commit, he cannot resist one last exercise
of his cunning.

Both Ulysses and Guido are undone. Ulysses, the
pagan, trusted in his own powers. They brought success
in the great enterprise against Troy, but failed him in
the end. Guido, the Christian, put his trust in the
misuse of his office by a rogue pope. He believed
Boniface's claim to have "the power to lock and to
unlock Heaven".[49] But Heaven is barred to Guido. For
Dante-Author the papal power to loose and bind is a
power to open the gates of Heaven to men by calling
them to their spiritual end. It is not an absolute,
unlimited power to admit the unrepentant and exclude
the righteous. Neither Ulysses nor Guido (not to
mention Boniface) looked beyond man to God. Indeed,
Ulysses and Guido each used his talents to subvert one
of these two great public institutions, Empire and
Church, that God has ordained for man's guidance. As
George Holmes notes, Ulysses wooden horse brought about

----------

46. "Ulysses and Guido (_Inferno_ XXVI-XXVII)," _Dante_
_Studies_, XCI (1973), 69.

47. _Inferno_ XXVI, 97-99.

48. _Inferno_ XXVI, 112-120.

49. _Inferno_ XXVII, 103.

the defeat of the Trojans, "the ancestors of the imperial Romans"; and Guido, by aiding Boniface in his struggle against the Colonna cardinals, "promoted the diversion of the Church from its proper path to the pursuit of war against fellow Christians."[50] Guido and Ulysses represent man's power of action unscrupulously used, placed in the service not of God but of human willfulness. Both were men of talent; both misused their talents. Both gave counsel that, for all its immediate success, led not only to their own ill end, but brought harm to others as well.[51] For all its excitement and fascination, a life of action that contravenes the will of God leads only to misery, not happiness. In Purgatory and Paradise we will meet other men of action, men who have escaped the snares and pitfalls that have captured these two appealing but forever damned shades.

As Dante himself had been powerfully attracted to the life of political action, especially during the years around 1300, when the events of the Comedy take place, so Dante-Pilgrim is depicted as being fascinated by Guido and Ulysses. So intent is Dante-Pilgrim to see them "that if I had not taken hold of a rock I should have fallen below without a push."[52] Dante-Pilgrim's dangerous fascination with these two damned shades suggest that Dante-Author may be repudiating his own previous immersion in political affairs to the exclusion of a sufficiently serious concern for God.

In Canto XXVIII, Dante-Pilgrim finds a troop of people who have been horribly mutilated. These are the makers of discord, those who have disturbed the peace and unity of the world. Unlike Farinata of Canto X, the inhabitants of this pit are punished not simply for their attachment to a part rather than the Whole, but for having positively split human society asunder by their sowing of bloody discord. This is a greater depravity than the factionalism of Farinata, and is symbolized by its perpetrators being much deeper in Hell.

----------

50. Dante (Oxford: Oxford University Press, 1980), pp. 58-59.

51. Truscott, "Ulysses and Guido," p. 68.

52. Inferno XXVI, 44-45.

As Dante and Virgil pass still further down into
Hell, Virgil turns the conversation to earthly fame.
Since ambitious men, including public men, tend to
value fame highly, this is a subject of considerable
political importance. Virgil speaks of "fame in the
world" as "that which is craved for here."[53] Fame and
memory in the world are compatible with Hell, with
eternal misery. Nor does one have to be possessed of
virtues and to have performed great deeds to be
immortalized by fame. Dante-Pilgrim induces Griffolino
of Arezzo to tell his story with the words: "so that
your memory not pass from the minds of men in the
former world but live on under many suns, tell me who
you are and of what people."[54] Dante-Author fulfills
the promise, immortalizing Griffolino in The Divine
Comedy. Yet for all his lasting memory, Griffolino was
unimportant, a person of no outstanding qualities.
Lasting memory is compatible with earthly insignifi-
cance as well as eternal misery. But when the final
depth of Hell, Cocytus, is reached, the inhabitants of
this icy land desire not remembrance but anonymity.
Their treacherous deeds are so vile that they refuse to
identify themselves, and only through the malevolence
of their neighbors does Dante-Pilgrim learn who they
are. Yet this unwillingness to identify themselves
still stems from a concern for earthly reputation.
These shades fear that any account of their deeds and
their place deep in the bowels of Hell will do nothing
but harm their reputations.

Judecca, the very center of Hell, holds Satan,
frozen from the waist down in solid ice. In each of
his three mouths he chews a paramount sinner. Christ's
betrayer, Judas, is flanked on either side by the
treacherous slayers of the first Emperor, Julius
Caesar. This scene depicts all that is wrong with the
world. Satan, the complete personification of a will
that rejects God's will, is at the center of the
scene. From the three mouths of this foul rejection of
God's will extend parts of the figures of Brutus,
Cassius, and Judas. They represent the betrayal of the
institutions God has willed for man's guidance, Empire
and Church. The betrayers of Church and Empire are
treated symmetrically; each is swallowed by the God-
rejecting figure of Satan. As Empire and Church are

----------

53. Inferno XXXI, 125-127.

54. Inferno XXIX, 103-106.

parallel authorities on earth, having a common source of their authority in God, so are the betrayers of Empire and Church given similar treatment in Hell, being swallowed by their common lord, Satan.

By climbing along Satan's body, Dante and Virgil pass through the bottom of Hell (the center point of the earth). Then they return to the surface by a passage that leads to Purgatory. For the first time they see the stars, symbols of the eternal. Yet these same stars are used by earthly men to tell time. The interpenetration of the eternal and the temporal, symbolized by the stars, is a fundamental idea of Dante's poem.

Between the Inferno's first image of Dante-Pilgrim come to himself in a dark wood, and its last image of Satan gnawing on the half-swallowed forms of Brutus, Judas and Cassius, great development takes place. Literally, Dante-Pilgrim makes a journey through Hell. Morally, the Inferno depicts the beginning of the living soul's journey from misery to felicity. The starting point is the recognition of one's estrangement from God--coming to oneself in a dark wood where the straight way is lost. This recognition in itself carries a faint awareness of God. It carries the soul to the edge of the dark wood, to the vision of the delectable mountain behind which rises the sun. But the spiritual aspirations of the sinful soul are defeated by its own unacknowledged baser impulses, symbolized by the leopard, the lion, and the she-wolf. Before it can rise above its sinfulness, the soul must know what stains it. In the absence of an adequate political power to curb cupidity and cultivate virtue in man, the soul needs to explore the depths of its sinfulness to motivate it to acquire the self-discipline it needs to undertake the purgative process. In the soul's exploration of the successive depths of its sinfulness, reason and virtue (Virgil) in the service of divine grace (Beatrice) can guide and encourage the weak pilgrim soul (Dante-Pilgrim). The soul that has truly grasped its own sinfulness has used the vision of Hell and Satan as a means to grow. Such a soul is ready for its next step, wholehearted repentance, the steadfast will to throw off one's enslavement to cupidity and cleave instead to God's will. Only when disciplined will is available to actualize the spiritual aspirations of the intellect is the soul ready to begin purging itself of its stain.

Politically, the _Inferno_ explores the disorder of public life. Following the estimable but insufficient achievements of antiquity symbolized by the Castle of Nobleness, we are shown progressively greater instances of disorder. As the Noble Castle symbolizes political order inspired by purely human aspiration and virtue, so the City of Dis symbolizes political order devoid of those same qualities. The City of Dis is entirely given over to willfulness, self-seeking and the indulgence of man's perverse impulses. The City of Dis contains in its depths the malevolent anarchy of Cocytus, which culminates in the figure of Satan gnawing on the three chief sinners. The chief cause of political disorder is shown to be treachery against the institutions God has granted man for his guidance, Church and Empire. Just as the individual soul receives an education in what ails it by its journey through Hell, so the political man receives an education in what ails public life. These educations do not cease with the _Inferno_. They continue in the _Purgatorio_, but are subordinated to a new theme: purification.

# Chapter 4

## THE PURGATORIO

From Hell to Purgatory is a vast climb. From the darkness, the hopelessness, the constrictedness, the damnation of Hell, Dante and Virgil reach the openness, light, hope, and aspiration of Purgatory. The transition from Hell to Purgatory symbolically represents the repentance of the sinner, his wholehearted turning from the bondage of sin toward the light of God. The soul's state is now quite different from its previous condition. "It", notes A.F.G. Howell, "is turned to God instead of being turned away from Him; it longs above all else that its will may by degrees be conformed to God's will, and is eager to undergo any pain, so that this goal may be attained."[1]

Purgatory is a mountain in the middle of the watery hemisphere. Its lower slopes contain those who for one reason or another must wait before entering the terraces upon which the soul's actual purification takes place. A beautiful garden, the Garden of Eden, surmounts the seven terraces which constitute Purgatory proper. Each terrace purges one of the seven deadly sins, and teaches the virtue which is that sin's opposite.[2] On the first terrace, for example, pride is purged and humility acquired. Each of these sins is a type of perverted love,[3] each virtue an aspect of rightly-ordered love.

The soul's stay in Purgatory is not unending. When it has completed the process of reordering its loves, it is released from this realm. The judgment, no longer deflected by perverted love, is then free to direct the will to God, the true good. Will, judgment and desire coincide, giving man a freedom and integrity

----------

1. _Dante_, p. 81.

2. Thomas K. Swing, _The Fragile Leaves of the Sibyl: Dante's Master Plan_ (Westminster, Maryland: Newman Press, 1962), p. 17.

3. Auerbach, _Secular World_, p. 112.

which in his sinfulness he lacked. Its will now wholly conformed to God's will, the soul is ready to rise to heaven.[4]

Morally understood, the Purgatorio's subject is the reordering of the soul's loves, in this life, by repentant Christians. According to Gardner it "represents the moral purgatory of repentant sinners in this world; and has for subject man, by penance and good works, becoming free from the tyranny of vice, attaining to moral and intellectual freedom".[5] As the moral meaning of the Purgatorio deals with the reordering of the soul's loves, so its political meaning deals with the reordering of man's relations with his fellows. The shades of Purgatory make their rounds in company with one another, and support each other in their efforts. They are training to take their proper places in God's universal Empire, wherein they will live in harmony with their fellow citizens. As Dante ascends the mountain of Purgatory, the absorption of the shades in the disordered politics of earth diminishes.[6] Inspired by the task at hand, they have something positive to set against the gloomy vision of a world whose cupidity is effectively restrained by neither Empire nor Church. They continue to recognize earth's ills, but the souls of Purgatory are not disheartened, for they are striving towards a state wherein right order does hold sway. What is true of the souls in Purgatory is true of repentant sinners on earth. Without losing sight of earth's disorder, they are buoyed up by their recognition of an order whose foundation is God.

In Purgatory, the characters of Virgil and Dante-Pilgrim also begin to change. Virgil is now somewhat out of his element. He, like Dante, is here for the first time. Virgil, the representative of purely human power and purely natural virtue, is still a valued and

----------

4. Edward Moore, "Dante as a Religious Teacher," in Studies in Dante, II, (Oxford: Clarendon Press, 1899), p. 59.

5. Dante, 1923, p. 130.

6. "How the Commedia Was Born," in From Time to Eternity, ed. Thomas G. Bergin (New Haven: Yale University Press, 1967), p. 16.

useful companion, but he is no longer the nearly-sufficient guide he was in Hell. Since purgation leads to the fulfillment of man's natural capacities, to man's natural end, Virgil remains a fitting guide for Dante-Pilgrim. But as purification cannot be achieved by purely natural means, Virgil's guidance is necessarily supplemented by spiritual guidance, coming from repentant Christians, angels, dreams, and visions. The other repentant Christians symbolize the earthly Church seen as a fellowship of repentant sinners who, still living, help one another along the way of their pilgrimage from misery to felicity. Together they sing hymns and recite parts of the services of the Church. Angels, channels of divine grace,[7] assist Dante on his climb. Dreams and visions come to him, suggesting the soul's growing yet imperfect capacity for subjective spiritual understanding. Dante-Author's meaning is clear. Individuals need additional spiritual resources for this part of their journey; in public life the value of the Church is proclaimed. Dante-pilgrim too changes from what he was in the Inferno. From a sometimes fascinated, sometimes scornful observer of sin and its consequences, Dante-Pilgrim becomes himself a participant in the purgative process.[8] He grows in purity of will from the beginning of the Purgatorio to its end. While still not an entirely reliable spokesman for the views of Dante-Author, our pilgrim is steadily coming closer to the author's perspective.

The first shade Dante-Pilgrim and Virgil meet in Purgatory is the Roman Cato. Cato fought against Julius Caesar and for the continuation of the Roman Republic. A stoic of the strictest rectitude, he took his own life rather than acquiesce in the overthrow of the Republic and the extinction of liberty. It is his upright character and complete commitment to liberty that bring him to Purgatory (and not to Hell, where as a suicide and opponent of the Empire he might conceivably be). Cato's wholehearted espousal of freedom was the cause of his preferment, because, as Sinclair points out, "for Dante, public liberty and liberty of the soul are ultimately one."[9] In Monarchy Dante treats both the free judgment of the soul and the

----------

7. Swing, Fragile Leaves, p. 87.

8. Smith, Greatness, p. 53.

9. Purgatorio, p. 29.

political freedom of the citizen as forms of the same basic freedom: freedom from forces that lead one away from doing what is right and good. Cato is the keeper of Purgatory because he sought that freedom unreservedly. He indicates that the determination to be free from sin is a precondition of the purgative process, and that political freedom under a good regime is essential if public life is to lead to man's felicity.

Following Cato's instructions, Virgil bathes Dante's face to remove the grime of Hell, and girds his waist with a reed (symbolizing humility) plucked from the water's edge. Another reed immediately springs up to replace the one that was plucked. This indicates that unlike human goods which are scarce and consumable, spiritual good is available without limit.[10] When men's attention embraces only earthly goods such as power and fame, the resulting competition leads to conflict. But when their striving is for spiritual goods, because there is no scarcity, there is no need for conflict. This understanding helps explain the grounds for Dante's belief that, rather than being rivals, Pope and Emperor should aid each other. By fostering peace and virtue, the Emperor establishes an environment conducive to the Pope's promoting spiritual aspiration in his flock. By calling men's attention to goods which are not scarce and for which they need not compete, the Pope facilitates the Emperor's task of bringing earthly peace to mankind. Here we have evidence of a practical basis for cooperation between Pope and Emperor.

In Cantos III through V Dante and Virgil meet shades who in one way or another seriously neglected their religious duties. For this negligence they are punished. Each must spend a period of time, different for different offenses, in waiting, before entering Purgatory proper and commencing purification. In the meantime they inhabit the Ante-Purgatory that lies just below Purgatory on the lower slopes of the delectable mountain. Only the prayers of those still on earth can speed their entrance into Purgatory. In these cantos Dante-Author makes clear that repentance, rejecting one's bondage to sin and receiving the faith that orients one toward the light of God, is the precondition of entering Purgatory and passing beyond Purgatory to the Garden of Eden. The Garden of Eden symbolizes the

----------

10. See Whitfield, Dante and Virgil, pp. 44-45.

full development of man's natural powers, his achievement of his natural end. The Purgatorio thus holds
that spiritual virtue is necessary for the complete
attainment of man's natural end. If man's natural end
were attainable through purely natural virtue, then
Virgil would be in the Garden of Eden, for he was not
at all lacking in natural virtue. It was lack only of
the three Christian virtues, and especially faith, that
condemned him to Limbo.[11] Dante-Author here holds that
spiritual virtue is essential if men are to perfectly
enjoy their natural, temporal end.

In Canto VI Dante and Virgil meet the Mantuan poet
Sordello. Sordello rejoices in being able to greet a
fellow Mantuan (Virgil). The warmth of Sordello's
greeting leads Dante-Author to denounce the strife that
prevails in Italy. This outburst recalls the Banquet's
image of wretched Italy abandoned to her own direction,
where the horse of the human will courses over the
plain without its rider, the Emperor.[12]

Ah, Italy enslaved, hostel of misery, ship
without a pilot in great tempest, no princess
among the provinces but a brothel!   ....
Search, wretched one, round the shores of thy
seas, then look within thy bosom, if any part
of thee rejoice in peace. What avails that
Justinian refitted the reins [codified the
Roman law] if the saddle [the upholding of
the law by the Emperor] is empty?[13]

Dante blames this condition on the seizure of
temporal power by leading churchmen. Addressing himself to these prelates he remonstrates:

Ah, ye that should be devout and let Caesar
sit in the saddle if you gave good heed to
God's direction to you, see how this beast
[Italy] has turned vicious for lack of

----------

11. Purgatorio VII, 7-8, 34-36.

12. Convivio IV. 9.

13. Purgatorio VI, 76-78, 85-89.

correction by the spurs since you laid hold
of the bridle.[14]

He fiercely rebukes the Emperor Albert for allowing
cupidity to distract him from reestablishing Imperial
authority in Italy:

> O German Albert, who abandonest her [Italy]
> that is become untamed and savage and
> shouldst bestride her saddle-bow, just
> judgment from the stars fall upon thy blood
> and be it so strange and manifest that thy
> successor may have fear of it. For thou and
> thy father, held back yonder by greed, have
> suffered the garden of the Empire Italy to
> be desolate.[15]

Here Dante states explicitly and unmistakably what he
often states indirectly in the Comedy: the cause of
the world's disorder is cupidity, affecting both Church
and Empire. When churchmen seek temporal aggrandizement, and emperors neglect their duty, order crumbles.
With furious invective Dante denounces this contempt by
Pope and Emperor alike for the order that God has
ordained.

Sordello explains to the travellers that no
progress toward Purgatory's summit is possible during
the dark, and leads them to the Valley of the Princes
to spend the night. Here Dante recognizes many recent-
ly-departed rulers, grouped together in one company.
As night falls, two angels appear to guard the band
against the attacks of a serpent.

This passage is significant. The alternation of
day and night, progressing and waiting, indicates the
pattern of the individual soul's journey. Only when
illumined by the light of God (the sun) can the soul
purge away part of its burden of sin. In its times of
difficulty, symbolized by darkness, progress is denied
it. At night the Valley of the Princes is attacked by
the serpent of temptation. The sincerely repentant
sinners that shelter there have the assistance of
divine grace (the angels) to protect them from temptation. After they enter Purgatory proper, the serpent

----------

14. Purgatorio VI, 91-96.

15. Purgatorio VI, 97-105.

56

will no longer have access to them. Then, although the penitents will still feel the attractions of the sins they are purging, these temptations will lack the venomous quality of the temptations of the Valley of Princes. The Valley of Princes symbolizes the state of living souls who have repented, but not yet begun the purificatory process. For them temptation is a real possibility of falling back into sin, whereas in Purgatory itself temptation is something recognized and willingly resisted in order to purify the will.

On the political level too this passage merits our attention. In contrast to the vivid depiction of factionalism in _Inferno_ X, here we see love displayed for a fellow citizen. Sordello's delight in meeting a fellow Mantuan stands in marked contrast to the Ghibelline Farinata's classifying Dante-Pilgrim as a political enemy, and overlooking entirely the presence in the same tomb with him of his Guelf fellow-citizen Cavalcanti. Yet bearing this in mind, Irma Brandeis reminds us that Sordello's love is still "touched with partisanship; it too, is based on a specific and restricting bond--on Mantua, and the 'glory of the Latins'.[16] It is a good beginning of love, but still too narrow." No more than Dante-Pilgrim has Sordello grasped the fact that all men are fellow citizens of God's universal empire.

The rulers who shelter in this valley have neglected their duties. Most were so caught up in their political ambitions that they delayed repentance until the last minute. At least one ruler, Henry III of England, appears to be here because he was so caught up in the performance of religious duties that he failed dismally as a temporal ruler. Collectively, these rulers failed to nurture peace and virtue in their subjects and in themselves. As a result of their (generally tardy) repentance they can see the three stars that symbolize the theological virtues of faith, hope, and love. But Dante goes out of his way to indicate that these rulers cannot see the four stars that stand for the natural virtues of courage, justice, wisdom and temperance,[17] the virtues they required to carry out their public responsibilities. Instead of

----------

16. _Ladder of Vision_, p. 79.

17. _Purgatorio_ VIII, 85-93.

bringing peace and virtue to their lands, they strug-
gled for supremacy amongst themselves. Now, however,
they know better. Old enemies comfort one another.
Voices which once were raised in discord now blend
harmoniously in the singing of an evening hymn.

Leaving Ante-Purgatory, Dante and Virgil pass
through the gate of Purgatory proper, "the gate which
the soul's perverse love disuses."[18] Dante-Author here
makes it clear that it is the soul's disordered love
that keeps man from reaching his natural and spiritual
ends (symbolized respectively by the Garden of Eden and
by Paradise). The gate to Purgatory is guarded by an
angel who has in his possession the keys to the Kingdom
of Heaven. "I hold them from Peter", he explains, "and
he bade me err rather in opening than in keeping
locked[19] if only the souls prostrate themselves at my
feet."[19] These are the keys to which Pope Boniface
VIII alluded in promising to absolve the monk Guido da
Montefeltro for the sin he would commit in advising
Boniface in his evil schemes. But for those who are
not truly repentant the keys do not turn rightly in the
lock, and the gate does not open. Guido is in Hell,
notwithstanding Boniface's claim. The angel with his
sword traces seven "p's" on Dante-Pilgrim's brow. Each
"p" is for one of the sins ("peccato") that is purged
in Purgatory. Each of Purgatory's seven terraces will
transform one kind of perverse love into its rightly-
ordered counterpart. As the soul ascends through the
terraces, reordering its loves, it loses one "p" for
each purgation it completes.

The first terrace purges pride. Here, as on all
the terraces of Purgatory, Dante and Virgil see examples of the virtue diametrically opposed to the sin
being purged. On this terrace where pride is expiated
they behold sculptures depicting humility. On every
terrace religious examples are augmented by an example
drawn from secular history.[20] Both spiritual and
secular virtue promote the soul's progress. The same
purgation of sin and growth of rightly-ordered love
leads to the natural felicity of the Garden of Eden as
leads to the supernatural felicity of Heaven. Growth

----------

18. Purgatorio X, 1-2.

19. Purgatorio IX,127-129.

20. Sinclair, Purgatorio, p. 140.

toward both man's temporal and spiritual ends is a single journey.

Among the souls atoning for pride, Dante and Virgil meet Oderisi, a famous illuminator of manuscripts. Oderisi now disparages the fame which on earth meant so much to him. He emphasizes its transience, its insubstantiality. "The world's noise is but a breath of wind which comes now this way and now that and changes name because it changes quarter."[21] "Your renown is the colour of grass which comes and goes, and that withers it [time] by which it springs green from the ground."[22] In evaluating this assessment of fame, we must recognize that Oderisi is acutely aware that his love of fame for its own sake got in the way of his loving God, the soul's true good. Here, on the first terrace of Purgatory, he is engaged in purging this sin of pride. In calling attention to the danger of loving fame he does speak for Dante-Author, but we should note that Oderisi's view is only a partial one. His devaluing of fame says less about its true value than it says about Oderisi's past weakness. Only in Heaven will we meet souls able to give true evaluations of the worth of earthly goods, including fame. Dante-Pilgrim, however, is greatly moved by Oderisi's words. "Thy true speech fills my heart with good humbleness and abates a great swelling in me."[23] Dante identifies himself with the souls who need to purge themselves of pride. He stoops down to their level and travels in company with them.

In the _Purgatorio_, Dante-Pilgrim no longer uses the promise of earthly fame to induce shades to tell their stories. The souls of Ante-Purgatory desire not fame but prayers of intercession on their behalf by persons still living, prayers whose effect will be to speed their entry into Purgatory proper. In Canto V, the late-repentant Jacopo del Cassero asks Dante-Pilgrim, should he ever see Jacopo's native city of Fano, "that thou do me the courtesy to beg them in

----------

21. _Purgatorio_ XI, 100-103.

22. _Purgatorio_ XI, 115-117.

23. _Purgatorio_ XI, 118-119.

Fano that good prayers be made for me, only that I may purge away my grievous sins."[24] In the Valley of the Princes, Judge Nino Visconti asks Dante-Pilgrim, when he is back on earth, to "tell my [daughter] Giovanna to plead for me there where answer is given to the innocent."[25] Unlike the inhabitants of Hell, whose aspirations were directed wholly toward transient earthly goods, the travellers through Purgatory seek loftier, spiritual goods. They have seen that there is a good greater by far than all earthly goods; this now is the focus of their aspiration. They have begun to see that earthly goods are good because they are part of the creation of the primary, eternal good, God. Recognizing this, they repent their sinfulness, their blindness, their bondage to desires whose intensity has obscured for them the true, supreme good.

Coming at last to the staircase to the second terrace, the angel who guards its entrance removes one of the "p's" from Dante's forehead. Dante-Pilgrim finds himself lighter and the climb easier. With its purgation on each successive terrace, the soul is lightened of its weight of sin, and finds the upward journey to God easier.

Reaching the terrace of envy, Dante inquires of the penitents here if any among them are Italian. He is told that here, all are citizens of the one true city. The factionalism of Farinata and the limited view of community possessed by Sordello have given way to a fuller understanding of man's citizenship.[26] In the one true city of God the earthly divisions that limit man's love for his fellows are transcended. This is dramatically illustrated in the case of Guido del Duca (a Ghibelline) and Rinier da Calboli (a Guelf). In striking contrast to Farinata and Cavalcanti in Inferno X, Guido and Rinier lean together and converse amicably.

As Dante and Virgil climb to the third terrace, that of anger, our attention is drawn to the differences between earthly and heavenly goods, earlier observed in the symbolism of the reed which, once

----------

24. Purgatorio V, 70-72.

25. Purgatorio VIII, 71-72.

26. See Brandeis, Ladder, p. 79.

60

plucked, was immediately replaced by another which sprang up in the same place.[27] In Canto XV Virgil states more directly that while earthly goods are scarce, heavenly goods are increased in proportion with the number who possess them.

It is because your desires are fixed where the part is lessened by sharing that envy blows the bellows to your sighs; but if the love of the highest sphere bent upward your longing, that fear would not be in your breast. For there, the more they are who say ours, the more of good does each possess and the more of charity burns in that cloister.[28]

Virgil does not claim to be able to explain completely why earthly and heavenly goods are so different. Still, he affirms them to be so and says that Beatrice will be able to give a fuller explanation. Here, as so often in Purgatory, Virgil is a reliable informant, but one whose explanations are only partial. Like the merely human knowledge on which they are based, his commentaries are valuable as far as they go, but they require something more; they need spiritual illumination to be complete. This spiritual illumination is beyond Virgil's powers to give, and beyond Dante-Pilgrim's capacity to receive at this stage of his journey. Only when he rises to meet Beatrice will he begin to gain more complete understanding.

On this terrace of anger Dante and Virgil encounter Marco Lombardo. Their meeting leads to an important discussion of the causes of the disorder evident in life on earth. Dante-Pilgrim inquires of Marco if it is the heavens, that is, forces beyond human control, that have produced such disorder, or does the responsibility lie with men? Marco, a penitent Christian, does not have the depth of knowledge on this subject that Beatrice will later display. His account of the matter is consistent with hers, however, and therefore should be understood as a reliable if incomplete statement of the views of Dante-Author. The heavens do indeed initiate many of men's impulses, Marco tells Dante, but free will "if it bear the strain

----------

27. Purgatorio I, 134-136.

28. Purgatorio XV, 49-57.

61

in the first battlings with the heavens, then, being rightly-nurtured, it conquers all." The stars do impart fundamental aspects of character to man, but free judgment can rightly order the will despite such influences. Since living men like Dante-Pilgrim have this capacity to develop their freedom of will, "therefore if the present world go astray, in you is the cause, in you let it be sought."[29]

The world is disordered because right nurturing is seldom given to the will on earth. Marco Lombardo explains that the newborn soul, in its ignorance, is unable to distinguish the relative values of different goods; without guidance it runs after trifling goods. "Therefore there was need for law to be set as a curb; there was need for a king who should discern at least the tower of the true city."[30] To discern at least the tower of the true city is an essential part of the lawmaker's job. On the basis of his vision of temporal felicity, he frames laws to discipline the will and lead mankind to earthly happiness.[31] The function of human law is thus to guide and nurture the ignorant soul. The laws exist (in the old Roman law) but they are not upheld, because the Pope's usurpation of temporal power has undermined the Empire's ability to enforce them. The Pope himself pursues goods other than the true good of God, setting an example that is followed by the multitude. "The people, therefore, who see their leader [the Pope] snatch only at that good for which they themselves are greedy worldly good , feed on that and ask for nothing more. Thus you can see plainly", Marco concludes, "that ill-guiding is the cause that has made the world wicked, and not nature that is corrupt in you."[32]

----------

29. Purgatorio XVI, 73-78, 82-83.

30. Purgatorio XVI, 94-96.

31. See Singleton, The Divine Comedy, Purgatorio, 2 Commentary, (Princeton: Princeton University Press: 1973), p. 363.

32. Purgatorio XVI, 97-105. See Singleton Divine Comedy, Purgatorio, 2 Commentary, p. 363-364; Grandgent, Dante Alighieri, pp. 256-257; D'Entrèves, Political Thinker, pp. 64-65.

To better attain their temporal and eternal ends, men need guidance from Empire and Church. "Rome", Marco asserts "which made the good world, used to have two suns [the Empire and the Church] which made plain the one way and the other, that of the world and that of God."[33] Of this passage Etienne Gilson writes: "the distinction between the road of the world and the road of God, each lightened by its own sun, is a faithful reflection of the distinction between the two final goals to which the Pope and Emperor lead humanity in the Monarchy."[34]

But the Church's usurpation of temporal authority has destroyed the conditions necessary for man's proper guidance. "The one [the Church] has quenched the other [the Empire] and the sword is joined with the crook, and the one together with other must perforce go ill, since, joined, the one does not fear the other."[35] Marco sums up his lesson in these words: "Tell henceforth that the Church of Rome, by confounding in itself two governments, falls in the mire and befouls both itself and its burden."[36]

Looking at human affairs from the third terrace of Purgatory, Dante-Author sees the Church as an important public institution. This is revealed by his treatment of Rome. In Monarchy Rome is the exemplar of secular, classical civilization. In Marco's speech, however, she is also a Christian city. One of her "two suns" is the Empire, but the other is certainly the Church.[37] Dante here and throughout the Comedy emphasizes the importance of the Church's influence upon the right-ordering (or ill-ordering) of the world.

----------

33. Purgatorio XVI, 106-108.

34. Dante the Philosopher, trans. David Moore (London: Sheeds and Ward, 1948), p. 307.

35. Purgatorio XVI, 109-112.

36. Purgatorio XVI, 127-129.

37. On Dante's emphasis on Rome as a Christian city, see D'Entrèves, Political Thinker, p. 65; Charles Till Davis, Dante and the idea of Rome (Oxford: Clarendon Press, 1957), p. 37.

Dante's emphasis on the Church goes hand in hand with his strong assertion of the rights and responsibilities of the Empire. The Empire too is needed for the world to be rightly ordered, and its jurisdiction must not be usurped by the Church. The two institutions should stimulate each other to greater efforts in their respective spheres. This is the meaning of Marco's Lombardo's assertion that "the one [the Church] together with the other [the power of the Empire] must perforce go ill, since, joined, the one does not fear the other." The strength of Dante's insistence on the independence of the Empire is seen in Marco's statement that the old Rome "which made the good world" had two suns. This two suns imagery is in striking contrast to the sun-moon analogy common in Dante's time. In the sun-moon analogy, which Dante himself uses in _Monarchy_, the Church is the sun and the Empire is the moon. The analogy was old and well-established. By replacing it with a two suns analogy, in which the Empire is a sun in its own right, Dante is deliberately asserting the coordinate status of the Empire.[38] Gilson puts the matter succinctly when he writes that not only is God the "keystone of Dante's system", but that "the Christian God of Dante is interested at least as much in protecting the Empire from the Church as in protecting the Church from the Empire."[39]

Approaching the fourth terrace, Dante-Pilgrim inquires what sin is purged here. Sloth, "the love of good which comes short of its duty," is Virgil's reply.[40] This leads to another important discussion, this time on the nature of love. Dante's theory of love is his psychological theory, his analysis of what leads men to act as they do. It is an important part of his political thinking. Virgil recognizes his limitations as an informant about love: "as far as reason sees here I can tell thee; beyond that wait only for Beatrice, for it is a matter of faith."[41] About

----------

38. See Kantorowicz, "Dante's Two Suns," in _Selected Studies_, p. 338.

39. _Dante the Philosopher_, p. 307.

40. _Purgatorio_ XVII, 85-86.

41. _Purgatorio_ XVIII, 46-48.

64

the origin of love, he says only: "neither Creator nor creature, my son, was ever without love."[42] Nor is he much more explicit about love's goal. "Everyone confusedly apprehends a good in which the mind may be at rest and desires it, so that each strives to reach it," he says.[43] But on the subject of how love operates, Virgil is more forthcoming.

> The mind, created quick to love, is readily
> moved towards everything that pleases, as
> soon as by the pleasure it is roused to
> action. Your perception takes from outward
> reality an impression and unfolds it within
> you, so that it makes the mind turn to it;
> and if the mind, so turned, inclines to it,
> that inclination is love, that is nature, by
> which pleasure is bound on you afresh. Then,
> as fire moves upward by its form, being born
> to mount where it most abides in its matter,
> so the mind thus seized enters into desire,
> which is a spiritual movement, and never
> rests till the thing loved makes it
> rejoice.[44]

In other words, perception derives from outward reality a mental impression, the unfolding of which draws the attention of the mind. If the mind is attracted rather than repelled, then this attraction is love. It is the nature of a mind possessed of love for an object to desire to attain the object. Parenthetically, Dante has told us that pleasure has the twofold function of binding the mind to the loved object and of rousing the mind to act to attain that object.

Love, depending on its object, brings happiness or misery. Love which "is directed on the primal good [God] and on the secondary [created things, goods other than God] keeps right measure...cannot be the cause of sinful pleasure."[45] Such rightly-ordered love leads to unalloyed felicity. Love of secondary goods is righteous or sinful depending on whether it leads to greater

----------

42. Purgatorio XVII, 91-92.

43. Purgatorio XVII, 127-129.

44. Purgatorio XVIII, 19-33.

45. Purgatorio XVII, 97-99.

or lesser appreciation of the primary Good. Dorothy Sayers asserts that when a love of secondary goods is rightly-ordered,

> it makes known the good things of this world
> as vehicles and sacraments of the Glory and,
> being directed through them to the Prime
> Good, leads to the Beatific Vision. When it
> is pursued disorderly and with a greedy
> excess, it makes of those goods only a
> series of mirrors reflecting the image of
> the Self, and leads to the 'Miserific
> Vision' of that which grinds its impotent
> teeth in the ice of Giudecca. All love of
> transient things is, essentially, of the one
> kind or the other, and tends, by little or
> much, in one of those two directions.[46]

Virgil tells Dante that when love "is warped to evil, or with more or less concern than is due pursues its goods, then against the Creator works His creature."[47] This is sin. Unrepented it leads to Hell, repented to Purgatory. The first three terraces of Purgatory, purging pride, envy, and anger, purge loves that have been warped to evil. The fourth terrace purges sluggish love of the prime Good, while the last three (those of avarice, gluttony, and lust) purge loves of secondary goods which have overshadowed the love of God. With the exception of sloth, the various sins consist in being caught up in loves (either evil or good) which hinder one's progress in fulfilling the primary desire, the enjoyment of the "good in which the mind may be at rest," the good of God.[48]

All sin is disordered love. All desires, including the loves that disturb the political world, the loves of power, wealth, fame and glory, are pursued because they seem to bring some good. Since it is the perception of good that triggers love, all loves seem blameless. Dante-Pilgrim wants to know if man is responsible for his loves.[49] Virgil replies that man's

----------

46. Further Papers, p. 144.

47. Purgatorio XVII, 100-102.

48. Purgatorio XVII, 127-128.

49. Purgatorio XVIII, 40-45.

"primal will" to find God is inherent in him; hence it [50] "admits no deserving of praise or blame."[50] Each individual, however, is responsible for controlling his other loves so that the highest good may be attained. Virgil explains:

> Now that in order to this primal will [the will to know God] every other may be conformed, there is innate in you the faculty which counsels and which ought to hold the threshold of assent [the faculty of judgement]. This is the principle in which is found the reason of desert in you according as it garners and winnows out good and guilty loves.[51]

In other words man is responsible for ordering his loves of secondary goods so that they support rather than hinder his love of the primary Good. His deliberative faculty should judge whether a particular desire is compatible with the primal desire, whether it should or should not be pursued.[52]

The Purgatorio dramatically illustrates the process of purification through which man's loves are put in order. Where this process leads is evident not from Virgil's speech but from the dramatic development of the poem. Love, when it is rightly ordered, leads to the Garden of Eden and thence to Heaven. The right ordering of love is how one makes the transition from misery to happiness.

Arriving at the terrace of avarice, Dante and Virgil meet Hugh Capet, who denounces the growing power of France in European affairs.[53] The views here expressed are undoubtedly those of Dante-Author, placed in the mouth of Hugh Capet, the founder of the ruling

----------

50. Purgatorio XVIII, 59-60.

51. Purgatorio XVIII, 61-66.

52. See Kenelm Foster, "Dante's Idea of Love," in Bergin, Time to Eternity, pp. 72-75, and Joseph A. Mazzeo, "Dante's Conception of Love," in Clements, Critical Essays, pp. 140-157.

53. Purgatorio XX, 40-96.

French dynasty, to heighten their impact. Sinclair succinctly summarizes Dante's views.

> For Dante the rising power of France, now
> predominant in Europe, defying and weakening
> the Empire, corrupting and enslaving the
> Church, intriguing and interfering by force
> and fraud in the affairs of Italy, was the
> public enemy of divine providence.[54]

Dante's treatment of France is significant because
it reveals his attitude to the growth of powers beyond
the control of either Church or Empire. He sees such
developments as further departures from the divinely
ordered pattern for life on earth. That pattern calls
for two guiding institutions for man, two suns in the
imagery of Purgatorio XVI. The eclipse of these two
suns by the rising planets of independent states was
for Dante yet further evidence of the disordered state
of the world. Not only has the sun of the Empire been
largely quenched by that of the Church, but both suns
are now less able to illuminate mankind because their
light is eclipsed by the rise of independent secular
kingdoms, especially France. Dante rued this development, but he recognized that it was happening. This
trend was to gather strength as the years went by until
the idea of a world guided primarily by the sister
institutions of Church and Empire was to become thor-
oughly implausible. Dante did not ignore what was
taking place, but, given his perspective, he could only
deplore it; it was caused purely by human ambition, and
took the world further and further from the unity so
essential to peace.

On this same terrace of avarice Virgil and Dante
meet the Roman poet Statius, who, as a repentant
Christian, has been in Purgatory for many centuries.
Only just before meeting Virgil and Dante has Statius
completed his purgation. He explains that as long as
one's sinfulness is not fully purged, one's desire
"sets to the torments as it was once set to the
sin."[55] Feeling attraction towards the sins they are
purging, the shades desire even more to be free from
sin's power to distract them from the true good, God.
The lives of these penitents are still disordered, but

----------

54. Purgatorio, p. 268.

55. Purgatorio XXI, 66.

68

they genuinely seek to set their loves in order. When this task is completed, their purified wills shall wholly conform to the will of God. Then, distracted neither by sinful loves nor by the necessary torments by which the will can alone be purified, their souls, free, pure, entirely at one with the will of God, shall rise to Paradise.[56]

From now on Dante-Pilgrim has two guides in his journey through Purgatory, Statius and Virgil. On the moral level of allegory, Virgil symbolizes the present value of ancient learning and virtue, and Statius represents the fellowship of living Christian saints. Politically Statius symbolizes the Church just as Virgil symbolizes the Empire. Statius shows great respect for Virgil. Not conflict but mutual esteem and confidence characterize the relationship between them. Again Dante-Author is affirming the value and compatibility of ancient learning and Christian sanctity, of temporal and spiritual guidance from Empire and Church respectively.

After passing through the ninth and final terrace of Purgatory the trio reach the end of Purgatory proper. Here Virgil bids farewell to Dante. Virgil's parting words make clear what his role has been.

The temporal fire [Hell] and the eternal
[Purgatory] thou hast seen, my son, and art
come to a part where of myself I discern no
further. I have brought thee here with
understanding and with skill. Take henceforth thy pleasure for guide. .... No longer
expect word or sign from me. Free, upright
and whole is thy will, and it were a fault
not to act on its bidding; therefore over
thyself I crown and mitre thee.[57]

Virgil's job has been to guide Dante-Pilgrim through Hell and Purgatory, to show Dante the consequences of disordered love and the process by which love is ordered aright. Virgil has been reason and philosophy acting at the bidding of grace (Beatrice). With Dante's love now rightly-ordered, reason and moral philosophy

----------

56. See Singleton, Divine Comedy, Purgatorio, 2 Commentary, p. 509.

57. Purgatorio XXVII, 127-131, 139-142.

are no longer needed to check the impulses of his will. His will is now truly free, free from being deflected from the true good by misdirected love. Dante can now take pleasure as his guide and follow his own will, unchecked by reason and philosophy, because his will is now perfected. It is not that he will defy reason and ethics; rather his will spontaneously and without prodding by Virgil chooses the right course. Nor does Dante-Pilgrim need the guidance of the Empire, also symbolized by Virgil. Law exists to guide and train weak, simple souls who have not yet set love in order. Dante-Pilgrim, having done this, no longer needs the Empire, at least for his own restraint. He is now his own guide. Virgil's words do not proclaim the demise of reason, philosophy, or the Empire. Rather they signify that Dante's soul has been purified to the point where it spontaneously and automatically acts in harmony with reason, philosophy, and law.

Because men are constantly being born into the world ignorant of the true values of its various goods there is constant need for external guidance, as symbolized by Virgil. But as individual souls make the transition from sinfulness to purity in this life, as they learn to will and to discern rightly, their need for external guidance finally disappears, and reason, philosophy, and law for these purified souls take on the different forms in which they appear in the Paradiso. Reason, philosophy, and the Empire will all be encountered in Heaven. But they will be transformed. Instead of being external guides to defective souls, reason, philosophy, and law will be internalized in souls whose wholeness and perfection of life find expression in their political and philosophical actions.

Having surmounted Purgatory proper, Dante-Pilgrim reaches the summit of the delectable mountain, followed by Virgil and Statius. Here Dante finds a lovely maiden picking flowers. Her name is Matilda, and she is the only permanent inhabitant of this fairest of all places found within time and space. This garden, located precisely on the top of the mountain of Purgatory, has rivers and breezes and fields and flowers. What distinguishes it from the rest of the earth is the purity of will of all who pass through it. It is an earthly place of unearthly tranquillity, a place wherein every will wills "Thy will be done."

This innocent, joyous place is Eden, the "place set apart to the human kind for its nest."[58] Here man was intended to live in the fulfillment of his natural capacities until God raised him to the supernatural felicity of Paradise.[59]

By his rebellion against God man was exiled from the garden. In exile he either lacks faith, or is enslaved by cupidity, or is engaged in the difficult task of purging himself of his disordered love. Whatever his condition, he cannot fully enjoy his natural capacities as God meant him to enjoy them. For man to regain this capacity, his will must be attuned to that of God. This is how Dante-Pilgrim and Statius have gained the garden of Eden, and it is clearly Dante-Author's intention to tell us that this is the only way Eden can be gained. Attuning one's will to that of God requires not only human effort, but also divine grace for its accomplishment. Virgil acts at the command of Beatrice; this is the formula that leads to the garden where man's natural capacities are fulfilled. Without Beatrice, without divine grace, Virgil, with his human learning, his human virtue, and his temporal Empire, leads only to the noble castle of Inferno IV. That castle is luminous but subterranean, filled with men and women who were noble but deficient in faith. By contrast the Garden of Eden is elevated, directly illumined by the sun and the stars; it is not just a globe of light in a region of darkness. Alone, human virtue leads at best to Limbo, to the incomplete fulfillment of man's natural powers. But when God's grace, received by men of faith, supplements natural human virtue, the road to Eden, to the perfect exercise of these powers, is opened.

The cantos dealing with God's earthly garden, like the rest of the Comedy, deal with man's life here on earth. Eden symbolizes the state in this life of those who have purged themselves of disordered love and have united their wills with God's will, but who have not yet received the spiritual illumination that is the subject of the Paradiso. As yet they act strictly with

----------

58. Purgatorio XXVIII, 77-78.

59. Purgatorio XXVIII, 92-93. See Singleton, Divine Comedy, Purgatorio, 2 Commentary, p. 680 and P.H. Wicksteed, Dante and Aquinas (New York: Haskel House, 1971, c. 1913) p. 219.

their natural powers, but in accord with the will of
God.

Eden is a necessary and worthy stop on the journey
of pilgrims from misery to happiness, from damnation to
reunion with God. Philip Wicksteed notes that "they
pass to the Celestial Paradise and enjoy the fruition
of the Divine Aspect only when they have first enjoyed
the fullness of earthly bliss as the original purpose
of the Creator planned." In appreciating this scene we
need to recall "the significance attached by Dante to
earthly life, regarded as having its own independent
significance and value, and as being worthy to be lived
and experienced for its own beauty."[60] While the perfection of the will that gives entry to Eden is not the
culmination of man's pilgrimage, it does permit him to
enjoy the full flowering of his purely natural
capacities.

Matilda symbolizes this state of natural fulfillment. She picks flowers which grow in the peaceful
garden. The picking of the flowers symbolizes enjoying
the rewards of a life of action. As she walks along
picking flowers,[61] she sings praises to God for the work
of His hands, the secondary goods which can be fully
and freely enjoyed now that the will is firmly united
with God. In the full realization of her natural
powers, she loves the Creator who made His creatures to
enjoy such natural, earthly felicity.[62] Her actions
are spontaneous expressions of the attunement of her
will to that of her Creator. To Edmund Gardner Matilda
represents "love rightly ordered and inflamed by divine
inspiration; awaiting the mystical ascent to the vision
and fruition of God."[63] In exercising her natural
powers in accord with God's will, her happiness is
representative of the felicity that man experiences in
attaining his temporal end.

----------

60. Dante and Aquinas, pp. 214-215.

61. Purgatorio XXVIII, 40-42.

62. See Singleton, Divine Comedy, Purgatorio,
2 Commentary, pp. 677-679.

63. Dante and the Mystics (New York: Octagon, 1968,
c. 1913), p. 270.

The achievement of man's natural end is
fillment but not a terminus. Matilda points
herself. She directs Dante's attention to the
of Revelation taking place at the other side      ~ne
river Lethe. The center of the pageant is a triumphal
car representing the Church, drawn by a griffin symbolizing Christ. Dante discerns riding on the car a
beautiful veiled lady, whose approach fills him with
trembling. His long-awaited reunion with Beatrice is
at hand. In his distress he turns to Virgil once more
for comfort, but Virgil is not there. Thus far he has
accompanied Dante, but with the appearance of Beatrice,
Virgil can come no more. Beatrice represents a more
than natural, more than temporal, more than rational
side of things. Virgil, while he can assist Dante in
getting to Beatrice, cannot help him in his actual
encounter with her.

Already filled with awe and trembling at the sight
of Beatrice, Dante weeps at the loss of Virgil.
Beatrice tells him not to weep for Virgil; he has
other, more important thing to weep for. She greets
him not as a purified soul, but as the lost, sinful,
miserable creature who emerged from the dark wood only[64]
to be driven back to it by the she-wolf. Before the
assemblage Beatrice accuses Dante of abandoning her.
"For a time", she says, "I sustained him with my
countenance. Showing him my youthful eyes I brought
him with me, bound on the right way." But with her
death, and despite her appearing to him in dreams and
other ways, "he took himself from me and gave himself
to another. When I had risen from flesh to spirit and
beauty and virtue had increased in me I was less dear
to him and less welcome and he bent his steps in a way
not true, following after false images of good which
fulfill no promise."[65] Beatrice tells Dante that
before he can pass through the River Lethe which erases
the memory of sin, he must first weep for the full
enormity of his sin.

Beatrice's indictment of Dante is significant,
both morally and politically. In abandoning Beatrice,
Dante abandoned not only the actual woman of that name
but also the revelation of God that she was for him.

----------

64. Brandeis, Ladder, p. 113.

65. Purgatorio XXX, 121-132.

He involved himself with other women, with philosophy, and with politics, to such an extent that the straight way was lost and he found himself in the dark wood. His excessive love of secondary goods, in other words, entirely obscured the vision of the primary Good which Beatrice had inspired in him. Of the secondary goods which proved so attractive to Dante some were of largely individual significance (women, for example), but one, political life, is important for our understanding of Dante's political thought. Dante here is warning against an absorption in secondary goods, including the good of participation in civic life, to the exclusion of the primary Good. There is no evidence that Dante-Author wanted to devalue the love of women, of philosophy, or of political life. But he does emphatically assert that, should they blind one to the primary good of God, they can be utterly damning.

Some commentators have taken this passage to advocate the abandonment of this world and its secondary goods in favor of the supernatural, eternal world.[66] But Dante-Author does not draw rigid boundaries between the natural and the supernatural, the temporal and the eternal. The two realms interpenetrate, and there is no conflict between earthly and spiritual goods for a soul which has ordered them rightly, and sees in earthly goods the reflection of their divine Creator. Philip Wicksteed penetrates into Dante's meaning when he writes that

> every student of the 'Comedy' has noticed the
> systematic parallelism between the sacred and
> secular examples of virtue and vice, and
> Dante's steady assertion of the intrinsic
> worth of the secular life. The history of
> Rome...is a sacred history no less than that
> of Palestine.... And this is not a secular-
> izing of the spiritual but a spiritualizing
> of the secular order of things. It is a
> systematic attempt to raise this life to the
> dignity and beauty of Eden, which in Dante's
> view was not merely a preliminary to the life
> of heaven, but an integral part of God's

---------

66. See, for example, Whitfield, <u>Dante and Virgil</u>, pp. 94-97.

scheme for man and a part which was worthily associated with the other.[67]

Following Dante-Pilgrim's confession, his weeping, his remorse, Matilda takes him across the river Lethe. Its waters wash away all memory of sin, all memory of estrangement from God's will. Dante is now much closer to Beatrice. Her revelatory role for him is restored. In her unveiled eyes he sees the two-fold nature of the griffin, human and divine. The pageant continues, only to end in tragedy. The triumphal car is attacked by an eagle, symbolizing the persecution of the Church by the Empire under the Emperors Nero and Domitian.[68] Next a dragon (heresy) attacks the car, rips away part of its floor, and wanders off. The eagle returns to what is left of the car and covers it with its plumage. This symbolizes the Donation of Constantine. Once the car acquires the Imperial plumage it undergoes a monstrous metamorphosis. An ungirt harlot surmounts the deformed chariot that once carried Beatrice. The harlot embraces a brutish giant, but her roving eye leads him to beat her and drag her into the woods. The Church (the truimphal car) is here depicted as being corrupted by its acquisition of temporal power (the plumage of the eagle), while its corrupt head (the harlot) is carried into captivity by the French king (the giant).[69] Beatrice prophesies the recovery of the Empire from its weakened condition. The _Purgatorio_ ends with Matilda taking Dante-Pilgrim across the river Eunoe, whose crossing restores the memory of every good deed. Its crossing symbolizes as well the readiness of the eye of the mind to receive the spiritual illumination that the ascent to Heaven brings.

The crossing of the Eunoe is an important one. It demonstrates that the enjoyment of God's natural garden is the fulfillment of only one aspect of man's nature. An even greater fulfillment awaits him. Entry to the garden is gained only by rightly-ordering one's loves, so that one's will is congruent with God's will. Once established in this state one spontaneously acts rightly, in accord with God's will, and in so doing enjoys the full flowering of one's purely natural capacities.

----------

67. _Dante and Aquinas_, pp. 134-135.

68. Sinclair, _Purgatorio_, p. 431.

69. See Sinclair, _Purgatorio_, pp. 431-432.

But this restored Eden is not the culmination of the journey. The Garden of Eden contains only the "first-fruits of eternal happiness".[70] Instigated by grace (Beatrice), right action (Matilda) prepares us for the heaven of spiritual illumination by purging even the memory of sin and restoring the remembrance of every good deed. The joys of utilizing man's purely natural powers in accord with God's will are enriched by the illumination that comes only with the development of spiritual insight. Consequently the life of action (which includes the life of political action) finds its ultimate fulfillment not in Eden but in Heaven.[71]

The individual or moral significance of the garden scene is to depict a particular stage in the spiritual development of the individual, a period after the will has been purified but before the conferring of intellectual illumination. The political significance of the scene is twofold. First, it shows that action in accord with God's will is possible for man and brings with it the joy of fulfilling one's natural capacities, including the capacity to enjoy earthly, secondary goods. Second, the disastrous ending of the Pageant of Revelation reiterates Dante-Author's contention that the exercise of temporal power by the Church is the root cause of the world's present disorder.

As a major unit within the Divine Comedy the Purgatorio literally depicts the state after death of penitent souls on their way to Heaven. Symbolically Ante-Purgatory illustrates the slow spiritual progress in this life of those who have neglected their religious duties. Purgatory proper displays souls in this life setting their loves and wills in order by steadfastly, and in company with other Christian souls, resisting the temptations that have previously ensnared them. The Garden of Eden shows the felicity of living men whose wills and loves have been purified so that they can now fully enjoy the exercise of their natural powers in earthly activity.

Politically, the Purgatorio chiefly deals with the relations of what should be man's two great guides in earthly life, the Church and the Empire. In the Purgatorio Dante has a high and positive view of both

----------

70. Purgatorio XXIX, 31-32.

71. Sayers, Introductory Papers, p. 117.

76

institutions, not, admittedly, in their present corrupt forms, but in their proper places within the divine order. Each should support the other. By directing men's aspirations toward plentiful spiritual goods, goods for which men need not compete, the Church can ease the Empire's task of bringing peace and order to social and political life. By upholding the law, the Empire disciplines the simple souls of men and restrains their often excessive loves of trifling goods. This is an important step, both for the gaining of temporal and eternal happiness, and for the proper ordering of human relations on earth. Furthermore, the two institutions should invigorate each other; the fear of the other can help keep each up to the mark. Etienne Gilson's remark, made in the context of a discussion of the Monarchy, is even more fitting when applied to the relations of Church and Empire in the Purgatorio: "what characterizes Dante's ideal is his deep faith that the works of God will harmonize provided that they remain true to their nature."[72]

The Purgatorio holds that man's nature has two aspects (natural and spiritual), two ends (temporal and eternal), and two guiding institutions (Empire and Church). The ends remain distinct. The institutions and their spheres of activity remain distinct. What must develop simultaneously are man's moral nature (his learning to curb his appetites) and his spiritual nature (his learning to love God above all lesser goods). Only the development of both aspects of man's nature leads through Purgatory to the Garden of Eden and to Heaven. The dramatic movement of the poem thus demonstrates the need for men to develop both aspects of their nature if they are to attain either of their ends. Since each institution, Church and Empire, specializes in the development of one aspect of man's nature, both institutions are needed, and neither has cause to usurp the functions of the other.

A second major political theme of the Purgatorio is its treatment of the causes of the world's disorder. When one institution does usurp the other's function, then the world goes astray. In particular, the present cause of the world's ills is the Church's usurpation of temporal authority. The Church has thereby weakened the Empire, which cannot properly uphold the law or keep in check the ambitions of

----------

72. Dante the Philosopher, p. 222.

temporal kings. Consequently both Church and Empire have been eclipsed by the power of independent national states. France is singled out for special mention here. With Church and Empire unable to adequately perform their duties, their influences are conspicuously absent from the place where they ought to be felt, in the purgatory of this earth. Here living men and women have to attempt the purification of their wills devoid of the help of the institutions that should be aiding them.

The third politically significant theme of the Purgatorio is its treatment of love, its analysis of what makes people act at they do. The Purgatorio states that men are responsible for rightly ordering their loves to facilitate rather than retard their journey toward the primary good of God. Since newborn souls lack knowledge of the true ordering of goods, they stand in need of guidance. The Empire, through its enforcement of laws that promote the development of virtuous living, can provide valuable guidance here. While the political thought of the Divine Comedy will not be completely expounded until the conclusion of the Paradiso, we now have a significantly greater appreciation of its political message.

# Chapter 5

## THE PARADISO

The _Purgatorio_ has considered how the will, once disordered, comes to love rightly, leading man to the full enjoyment of his natural capacities. The _Paradiso_ portrays the supernatural intellectual illumination that ensues, an illumination which transcends that available through the exercise of man's purely natural capacities. This spiritual illumination follows the soul's right-ordering because it is essentially a vision of the order of the Whole. A soul estranged from God cannot discern this order; but once attuned to God, the soul can begin to recognize the Whole of which it is a part.

Although its literal story line brings Dante-Pilgrim into contact with souls in the afterlife, the _Paradiso_, in common with the rest of the _Comedy_, is concerned with men and women in this life. Dante is telling us that living men and women, in addition to attaining their temporal end (symbolized by the Garden of Eden) can also rise to their eternal end (symbolized by Paradise). Even in this life the divine gift of spiritual illumination can be enjoyed.[1] "This vision of the whole, without diversity or contradiction, is a divine gift", writes Dorothy Sayers. "It does not belong to human nature--not even to human nature in its original perfection--but is something superadded. Nature must not indeed be lost in order to attain vision, but it must be 'transhumanized'."[2] The moral and political consequences of this ascension, this "passing beyond humanity",[3] are elucidated in this the final book of the _Comedy_.

To communicate his vision of the Whole, Dante-Author has his pilgrim meet different souls in Heaven.

----------

1. See Singleton, _Dante Studies I: Commedia, Elements of Structure_ (Cambridge: Harvard University Press, 1954), pp. 3-4. See also Singleton, "Dante's Allegory," _Speculum_, XXV (1950), 81-83.

2. _Introductory Papers_, p. 180.

3. _Paradiso_ I, 70

These illumined souls are truly <u>citizens</u> of Paradise; they are joyful participants in the heavenly order. They all enjoy the vision of the Whole, for they dwell in the immediate presence of God. Each heavenly soul is fitted by its earthly experience and heavenly illumination to speak authoritatively about some aspect of the Whole. The Beatific Vision itself, which reveals to the intellect the full coherence of the Whole, is indescribable.[4] But individual souls can describe their own areas of special competence in light of the Whole; their descriptions indirectly communicate a sense of that Whole to the reader.

The dramatic action of the <u>Paradiso</u> consists in Dante-Pilgrim's ascension from the Garden of Eden through the celestial heavens to the ultimate heaven, the Empyrean, where he experiences the Beatific Vision. The various heavens are portrayed as a series of concentric spheres circling the Earth. Nearest Earth is the heaven of the Moon, then those of Mercury, Venus, the Sun, Mars, Jupiter, Saturn, and the fixed stars. Beyond even the fixed stars lies the Primum Mobile, a transparent, invisible sphere whose infinite velocity of rotation is the source of the motion of the lower heavens. Beyond the Primum Mobile, beyond space and time completely, is the Empyrean. This is the true home of the blessed souls Dante-Pilgrim meets in Paradise. But while the Empyrean is their true home, they have come down to meet Dante in the spheres appropriate to their natures. In each sphere Dante-Pilgrim meets illumined souls of a particular character, souls whose experience has fitted them to speak authoritatively about one aspect of the Whole. In Heaven, as in Hell and Purgatory, Dante-Pilgrim is only a visitor. He cannot remain in Paradise; he must return to earth, to inform his fellow men of his discoveries, and to inspire them to reform their lives.

In Canto I Dante-Pilgrim rises from Eden to the first sphere. His ascension comes from looking at the eyes of Beatrice, from giving his full attention to revelation and divine grace. "At her aspect I was changed within.... The passing beyond humanity cannot be set forth in words."[5] The spiritualization of Dante-Pilgrim has begun. He, however, is surprised and

----------

4. <u>Paradiso</u> I, 6-9.

5. <u>Paradiso</u> I, 67-71.

confused. Seeing his perplexity, Beatrice explains
that God has so ordered His universe that in it the
rightly-ordered soul is as inclined to ascend toward
God as a stream is inclined to fall "from a mountain
height to the foot."[6] While the divine grace that
lifts the soul to heights of spiritual illumination is
supernatural, it is not contrary to nature. The
natural and the supernatural unite to form a single
consistent Whole. The opening words of the Paradiso,
spoken by Dante-Author directly to the reader, proclaim
the supernatural presence of God throughout his natural
universe. "The glory of Him who moves all things
penetrates the universe and shines in one part more and
in another less."[7] The natural and the supernatural,
the material and the spiritual, are both integral parts
of God's creation. How they are related Beatrice will
explain more fully in Canto II.

The progressive illumination of the intellect of
the grace-infused soul is symbolized by the progressive
illumination of the intellect of Dante-Pilgrim. In the
early cantos of the Paradiso Dante-Pilgrim is perplexed
in this spiritual realm. He needs the revelatory grace
of Beatrice to further enlighten his understanding. As
he ascends in his journey, his spiritual awareness
increases until he experiences directly the Light
Eternal which memory cannot hold nor words describe.
In this life, Dante-Author is telling us, spiritual
experience is at first unexpected and confusing, but in
time and with further growth it becomes clear.

In Canto II Beatrice expounds to Dante the operation of the heavens. Dante-Pilgrim has put forward a
physical explanation of a heavenly phenomenon, only to
have Beatrice refute it. Beatrice does not deny that
there is a material element to the heavens, but she
emphasizes that they and their operations derive from a
spiritual cause. Singleton succinctly summarizes the
substance and significance of her explanation thus:

> The outermost of the material heavens, the
> Primum Mobile, derives a "virtue" (power)
> from the spiritual heaven [the Empyrean]
> which contains it, and it in turns transmits
> this power to the material universe which

----------

6. Paradiso I, 138.

7. Paradiso I, 1-3.

lies within it; and in this way we begin to
follow out the passing down through the
spheres of a power which, in its origin, is
spiritual, is from God.[8]

The universe is simultaneously spiritual and physical.[9] Each sphere is controlled by a particular order
of intelligences (angels) who impart to it its distinct
characteristics. The material and the spiritual interpenetrate.

The first heaven Dante-Pilgrim experiences is that
of the Moon. The Moon is the least of the heavens, the
lowest, slowest moving, and farthest from the Primum
Mobile. Here, in this lowest heaven, Dante meets
Piccarda Donati. She explains that their meeting in
the lowly sphere of the Moon indicates her low rank in
the heavenly court. She ranks no higher, she says,
because of her neglect of her earthly vows. Still, she
is content with her place in Heaven. Her will entirely
conformed to that of God, she rejoices to occupy that
place in the heavenly order that He has willed for
her. Dante-Author remarks "it was clear to me then
that everywhere in heaven is Paradise, although the
grace of the Supreme Good does not rain there is one
measure."[10] The meaning of this discovery for earthly
life is clear. In this life too spiritual illumination
comes in different measures to different persons, according to their deserts. All rightly-ordered souls,
however, are content with that measure of illumination
with which they are blessed.[11] Dante asks Piccarda if
she is not dissatisfied with her low place in heaven;
she explains that such dissatisfaction is impossible,
contrary to the essence of the heavenly state. She
gives Dante an essential explanation:

----------

8. The Divine Comedy, Paradiso, 2 Commentary (Princeton: Princeton University Press, 1975), p. 56.

9. Sinclair, Paradiso, p. 46.

10. Paradiso III, 88-90.

11. See Charles H. Grandgent, La Divina Commedia di
Dante Alighieri (revised ed.; Boston and New York:
Heath, 1933), p. 648.

it is the very quality of this blessed state
that we keep ourselves within the divine
will, so that our wills are themselves made
one; therefore our rank from height to height
through this kingdom is pleasing to the whole
kingdom, as to the King who wills us to His
will. And in His will is our peace. It is
that sea to which all things move....[12]

Piccarda speaks here for all of Heaven's citizens.
Despite their differences, they all concur in willing
God's will. They all find that "in His will is our
peace."

Peace was something for which Dante deeply longed,
perhaps because he saw so little of it in Italy. Peace
is to be desired in both its spiritual and temporal
aspects. The peace of which Piccarda speaks is clearly
spiritual peace, the peace of a soul at one with its
Creator. But for Dante all peace, temporal as well as
spiritual, comes from God. In Monarchy he writes that
the shepherds at Bethlehem announced to the world not
wealth or honor or any other worldly good, but universal peace.[13] Peace on earth comes ultimately from
Heaven.

Terrestrial and spiritual peace are achieved in
similar ways. The earthly peace which the Monarchy
seeks requires that men's wills be united in the will
of a universal monarch.[14] The spiritual peace of
Heaven's citizens flows from their spontaneously
keeping themselves "within the divine will so that our
wills are themselves made one."[15] Piccarda's words
express the illumined intellect's recognition of the
need for man's will to be attuned to that of God, on
earth as in Heaven. While the unity of wills among
Heaven's citizens is spontaneous, earth's simple souls,

----------

12. Paradiso III, 79-86.

13. Monarchy I. 4.

14. Monarchy I. 15.

15. Paradiso III, 81.

83

when left to their own devices, avidly pursue a
multitude of inferior goods.[16] It is the task of the
Empire, through good laws, to tame man's unruly will,
direct it toward a life of virtuous action, bring it
into concord with other wills, and give man the
blessing of earthly peace. Similarly the Church's
function is to direct man's attention toward spiritual
goods and to encourage the soul's embrace of the divine
will, an embrace which brings spiritual peace.

In Canto IV Beatrice explains that the will's
attunement to God can be disrupted by external circum-
stances. Piccarda occupies a lowly place in Heaven
because, involuntarily taken from her convent, she
failed to flee back to it when the opportunity arose.
Her will, though attuned to God, was bent by external
force, and the measure of divine illumination granted
her is thus less than that granted those whose firmer
wills withstood the onslaught of unfavorable external
pressures. Beatrice contrasts Piccarda's weakness with
the strength of will shown by the Christian Saint
Lawrence and the Roman Mucius. Both Lawrence and
Mucius displayed a firmness of will that endured
despite terrible adversity. "So firm a will is rare
indeed," Beatrice says.[17]

Piccarda's character was also changeable. She
meets Dante in the sphere of the Moon, a body whose
astrological association is with inconstancy. Her
changeability, in conjunction with external force, kept
her from carrying out her religious vows. Her failing
was serious. It places her in the lowest rank of
Heaven's citizens, amongst those of the most limited
spiritual insight. Nevertheless, despite her past
weakness, in the end Piccarda ordered her will rightly
and God accordingly granted her the grace of divine
illumination. She shows no regret. From Piccarda's
story we learn that perfect attunement of the will to
God prepares one to receive heavenly illumination, but
defects of inborn character, which limit the force of
that will, limit the intensity of the soul's illumination. The illumination received is real and enduring
nonetheless.

----------

16. Purgatorio XVI, 91-93.

17. Paradiso IV, 87.

Also in Canto IV, the always truthful Beatrice explicitly informs Dante of the reliability of the words of the souls he meets in Heaven. "A soul in bliss cannot lie, since it is always near the primal truth."[18] As readers of Dante's great poem, we can thus accept the words of the blessed souls as valid expressions of the ideas of Dante-Author. We need not weigh the credibility of the characters as we have done for the _Inferno_ and the _Purgatorio_.

Through her gaze Beatrice raises Dante to the next heaven, Mercury. Here he meets the Emperor Justinian. As the codifier of the Roman law Justinian is uniquely qualified to discourse on the place of the Empire in the order of the Whole. He briefly but magisterially recounts the history of Rome, not as secular history but as sacred history. The Eagle, symbol of the Roman Empire, is "the bird of God".[19] Rome he calls "the most holy standard".[20] Rome's triumphs are God's triumphs, for the Roman Empire is divinely ordained. In sixty lines of the _Paradiso_ Dante-Author expounds the view he espouses in Book II of _Monarchy_: Rome gained her Empire by right and by God's express intention. Rome's Empire is God's Empire. In crucifying Christ, it played a divinely authorized role in the atonement. Justinian's proclaims:

> But what the standard that moves my speech
> [the Roman Empire] had done before and was
> yet to do throughout the mortal kingdom that
> is subject to it [the great deeds of the
> Empire done in its rightful domain], comes to
> seem small and dim if with clear eye and
> right affection we look at it [the Empire] in
> the hand of the third Caesar; for the Living
> Justice [God] that inspires me granted it, in
> his hand of whom I speak [the third Caesar,
> Tiberius], the glory of doing vengeance for
> His wrath [of punishing mankind for its
> disobedience to God through the crucifixion
> of Christ, who took mankind's sinfulness upon

----------

18. _Paradiso_ IV, 95-96.

19. _Paradiso_ VI, 4.

20. _Paradiso_ VI, 32.

Himself that in being punished for mankind,
He might reconcile God with man.] [21]

The Empire therefore is part of the order of the Whole.
It is willed by Divine Providence and is not merely the
consequence of the doings of ambitious men. The last
Emperor whose deeds are recounted by Justinian is
Charlemagne. By including Charlemagne amongst the
bearers of the most holy standard, Dante-Author indicates that the Holy Roman Empire of his day was,
ideally if not always in practice, the same divinely
ordained Empire that had conquered the ancient world.
The authority of the Empire has not passed away; it
still endures. [22]

Justinian, however, takes no sides in the quarrel
between Guelfs and Ghibellines. He rebukes them both.
He denounces the Guelfs for opposing the Empire and
supporting those flouters of imperial authority, the
kings of France. He denounces the Ghibellines for being
a mere faction. "Let the Ghibellines carry on their
arts under another standard," Justinian declares, "for
of this [the standard of the Empire] he is always a bad
follower who severs it from justice." [23] The Ghibellines are self-interested; they are not the true
servants of God's Empire they purport to be. Significantly, this sin of factionalism on the part of the
Ghibellines is the same one for which Dante condemned
the great Florentine Ghibelline, Farinata, to Hell. The
Empire is God's Empire, bringing peace and justice to
all men. It is not the cause of any self-serving
faction.

Dante insists that the God's Empire should be
Christian. In Canto VI of the _Paradiso_ Justinian
recounts how his relationship to Pope and Church came
to be one of receptivity to the Church's spiritual
teaching. Originally subscribing to a false understanding of the nature of Christ, Justinian says that
Pope Agapetus "directed me by his words to the true
faith. I believed him...." Then, "as soon as I took
my way beside the Church," God's inspiration came, and
Justinian, through his general Belisarius, undertook

----------

21. _Paradiso_ VI, 82-90.

22. See Sinclair, _Paradiso_, p. 95.

23. _Paradiso_ VI, 103-105.

the successful reconquest of Italy.[24]  Justinian took
his way beside, and not behind, the Church.  While in
spiritual matters the Emperor is receptive to the
teaching of the Pope, Pope and Emperor are coordinate
authorities, equal and unchallenged each within his own
area of activity.  Justinian's example illustrates the
independent but cooperative relations between Church
and Empire that Dante advocates.

        Justinian, like Piccarda, ranks low in Heaven.  He
meets Dante in the sphere of Mercury, the second lowest
heaven, a planet whose influence produces sharpness of
intellect directed toward earthly ends.[25]  Dante thinks
that Justinian's sharp intellect codified the Roman
law, the law of the Empire, the basis of civil peace
and justice.  But Justinian carried out his great works
with an eye to earthly honor and glory.  He meets Dante-
Pilgrim in Mercury, amidst the souls of Christians
"whose deeds were done for the honor and glory that
should follow them."[26]  Because some of his love mounts
up to God only indirectly, via the secondary good of
fame, "the rays of Justinian's true love [for God]
must needs mount upward with less life."[27]  Allegori-
cally, love of honor and glory does not preclude
spiritual illumination, but can limit its intensity.

        Love of honor and glory is compatible with spiri-
tual illumination if it impels one to act in accordance
with God's will.  The Roman greats whose deeds are
recounted by Justinian loved glory.  But since their
deeds furthered God's Empire, they served God's will.
Hence, for all their love of glory they could know
spiritual illumination provided they were men of
faith.  Justinian himself was one such person.  This
contention that the love of honor and glory can serve
God's ends is seen also in Inferno XXIV, where Dante-
Pilgrim is discouraged.[28]  Virgil, acting at the behest

----------

24. Paradiso VI, 13-27.

25. Helen Flanders Dunbar, Symbolism in Medieval
Thought and its Consumation in the Divine Comedy (New
York: Russell and Russell, 1961, c. 1929), p. 45.

26. Paradiso VI, 113-114.

27. Paradiso VI, 116-117.

28. lines 46ff.

of divine grace (Beatrice) exhorts Dante to cast off sloth in order to achieve fame. The love of fame is used to inspire acts ordained to a heavenly purpose.

In Canto VII Dante further develops his theory of love, stating the matter directly and succinctly. The speaker is Beatrice. She now fulfills Virgil's promise in _Purgatorio_ XVIII that Beatrice would explain the origin of love, a subject beyond Virgil's understanding. Beatrice informs Dante-Pilgrim that love comes from God. "Your life the Supreme Beneficence breathes forth immediately, and He so enamours it of Himself that it desires Him ever after."[29] The human soul proceeds directly from God, who breathes it forth immediately and directly. This original, direct contact of the soul with God kindles in it the desire to return to its Creator. Whatever lesser loves the soul may espouse in its journey, its ultimate desire is for reunion with Him. Love originates and culminates with God.[30]

In Canto VIII Dante and Beatrice rise to the heaven of Venus, where Dante meets Charles Martel. Martel explains to Dante the influence of the stars in fixing the diverse natures of different men. The influence of the stars on human character is ultimately traceable to the workings of Divine Providence. Beatrice has already explained in Canto II how the power of the heavens derives ultimately from God. Charles Martel tells Dante that different qualities are infused into individual characters by the stars in keeping with God's plan for the well-being of his creatures. "Not only is the nature of things provided for in the Mind which has perfection in itself [God], but along with their nature their well-being." As a bow directs its arrow to the target, so God, through the planets, infuses into individual human natures the qualities necessary for individuals to play their parts in the divine plan.[31]

In the sphere of Venus, Dante also meets Cunizza and Folco. Like Charles Martel, they have the defect

----------

29. _Paradiso_ VII, 142-144.

30. For a thorough treatment of Dante's theory of love, see Foster, "Dante's Idea of Love," pp. 65-101.

31. _Paradiso_ VIII, 97-105.

of character that comes from being influenced by the morning star, an excessively amorous nature. Cunizza is reticent about her life. She says only that "I shine here because the light of this star overcame me...."[32] Folco admits to the same character in more flowery words. Neither regrets their nature. Cunizza tells Dante-Pilgrim: "I gladly pardon in myself the reason of my lot, and it does not grieve me."[33] Folco further explains why those Dante meets in the first three heavens do not regret their flawed characters. "Here we do not repent" he says, "nay, we smile, not for our fault, which does not come back to mind, but for the Power which ordained and foresaw."[34] Folco's assertion that their faults do not return to mind recalls the passage through the river Lethe in Eden.[35] In passing through Lethe, the purified soul loses all memory of sin, of estrangement from God's will. It no longer sees its temperament as sinful, because that temperament does not prevent the will's attunement to God.

All three of the souls with whom Dante converses in the heaven of Venus speak of earthly affairs. Cunizza denounces the violence, peacelessness and injustice of her native district.[36] Charles Martel explains that one reason for the ill success of earthly affairs is that men are often thrust into positions for which they are by nature unsuited. "You [earthly men] wrest to religion one born to gird on the sword, and you make a king of one that is fit for sermons, so that your track is off the road."[37] This simple statement is important. It helps explain why some churchmen seek temporal power and some temporal rulers lack the resoluteness of character required to uphold peace, law and justice. The Church thus acquires political power, and the Empire grows weak. While God has, through the

----------

32. Paradiso IX, 32-33.

33. Paradiso IX, 34-35.

34. Paradiso IX, 103-105.

35. Singleton, Divine Comedy, Paradiso, 2 Commentary, p. 170.

36. Paradiso IX, 43-60.

37. Paradiso VIII, 145-148.

stars, infused into different men the different natures required for the fulfillment of His divine plan, the world fails to make proper use of the natures found in it.

The world does not fully utilize its human resources in part because of the failure of the Church to perform its rightful function. Folco, a bishop, explains the Church's delinquency by pointing to the avarice of its high officers. The gold florin of Florence, the most prized currency of the age, he decries as "the accursed flower that has led astray the sheep and the lambs, for it has made a wolf of the shepherd."[38] Avarice has corrupted the people, the clergy, and, most significantly, the Popes. "For this [florins] the Gospel and the great Doctors [of the Church] are neglected."[39] With the Church failing to provide Christians with proper guidance it is hardly surprising that the world goes astray.

Rising from Venus to the heaven of the Sun, Dante-Pilgrim meets twelve shining spirits, the first of three groups of souls that will appear to him here. These spirits shine with a brighter intensity than those below. They are all men of wisdom. They represent the wisdom of the active (as opposed to the contemplative) life. "The sphere of the Sun" Dorothy Sayers writes, "is intended to give us a representative view of the active intellect in operation."[40] Amongst the figures Dante meets in this sphere are King Solomon, Saint Bonaventura, and Saint Thomas Aquinas.

Saint Thomas, the great Dominican, tells the story of the founder of the Franciscans, the great order that rivaled the Dominicans. But before he can do so, Dante-Author interjects to contrast the joys of spiritual illumination with the vain attempts of sinful men to find happiness in acquiring secondary goods at the expense of the Primary Good. This impassioned denunciation will be echoed in the speeches of Saint Thomas and Saint Bonaventura.

----------

38. Paradiso IX, 130-131.

39. Paradiso IX, 133-136.

40. Introductory Papers, p. 118.

O INSENSATE care of mortals, how vain are the
reasonings that make thee beat thy wings in
downward flight! One was going after law,
another after the Aphorisms [practicing
medicine], one following the priesthood and
another seeking to rule by force or craft,
one set on robbery and another on affairs of
state, one labouring in the toils of fleshy
delights and another given up to idleness;
while I set free from all these things, was
high in heaven with Beatrice, received thus
gloriously.[41]

The image of winged man asserts the possibility of
man's rising to enjoy higher goods, especially knowledge of God, spiritual illumination. But man applies
himself to the pursuit of lesser goods and ignores the
higher goods that God in his grace makes available to
him. In contrast to this bondage to the allurement of
lesser goods, Dante juxtaposes the picture of a soul
"free from all these things ... high in heaven with
Beatrice, received thus gloriously."

Some commentators see in this passage a repudia-
tion of Dante's concern for the active life. The
spiritual ideal kills the ideal of temporal beatitude.
Earthly life is without value. J. H. Whitfield, for
example, writes that "it is not the order of earthly
things which is wrong and must be changed; it is the
substance which is worthless and had better be abandoned."[42]

This, however, is not Dante's attitude. The thrust
of the Paradiso is rather to show the interpenetration
of the spiritual and the physical, the eternal and the
temporal. Dante does not attempt to separate them and
then exalt the spiritual while disparaging the earthly. What he denounces is placing secondary goods
before the primary good, God. This is sin, and leads
only to the misery depicted so vividly in the Inferno.
In the Paradiso, however, we encounter souls completely
attuned to God, living in the light of divine illumination. To such souls the secondary goods of earthly
life cannot possibly obscure the Primary Good. To them

----------

41. Paradiso XI, 1-12.

42. See Whitfield, Dante and Virgil, pp. 49-50.

the goods of earthly life are true goods, particular manifestations of the divine Goodness. The substance of earthly life is far from worthless, and not to be abandoned. Rather, as Dorothy Sayers points out, the first six heavens represent the perfection, not the demise, of the active life.[43] Dante's quarrel is precisely with the wrong ordering of earthly life, not with its substance.

This interpretation is confirmed by the dramatic movement of the poem in the two cantos immediately following Dante-Author's outburst. The vile disorder found on earth results from the corruption of the Church and not from any inherent worthlessness of earthly things. Saint Thomas Aquinas tells the story of the founder of the Franciscans, Saint Francis of Assisi, in such a way as to contrast Francis' unwavering marriage to poverty with the preoccupation of most contemporary Dominicans with gaining worldly goods. And in Canto XII the great Franciscan Saint Bonaventura recounts the life of the founder of the Dominicans, Saint Dominic. He contrasts Dominic's integrity of godly purpose with the avarice and worldly ambition of leading contemporary churchmen, and the divorce of most contemporary Franciscans from the poverty of their founder. Dante is not disparaging worldly enjoyments per se; he denounces rather the pursuit of worldly goods by those whose vocation calls for poverty. Dominated by men seeking wealth and power, the corruption of the Church is central to Dante's explanation of the ill-ordering of the world. The seeking after temporal power by the Popes weakened the Empire and kept it from providing men with temporal peace, law and justice. In seeking wealth, the great churchmen neglected their spiritual duties and set a bad example for the faithful. Bruno Nardi aptly notes: "to re-establish order on earth it was necessary not only to restore imperial authority but also to carry out a religious reform which would lead the Church back onto the straight path."[44] Nardi sees that for Dante it was the order rather than the substance of earthly life that was askew.

----------

43. Introductory Papers, p. 117.

44. "Dante and Medieval Culture," trans. Yvonne Freccero, in Dante: A Collection of Critical Essays, ed. John Freccero (Englewood Cliffs, N.J.: Prentice-Hall, 1965), p. 41.

If Dante calls on churchmen to renounce their campaign for wealth and power, so he calls on the Imperial authorities to turn aside from abstract philosophical speculation. King Solomon is praised for desiring the practical wisdom required by an earthly ruler rather than abstract philosophical knowledge.[45] Wise men should devote themselves wholeheartedly to that form of wisdom that is appropriately theirs, and not meddle in the domains of others. Churchmen should get out of political affairs, and perform instead their duties of spiritual leadership. Rulers should not attempt to philosophize but should devote themselves to the practical task of bringing peace and justice to their subjects.[46]

From the sphere of the Sun Beatrice and Dante rise to the heaven of Mars. Here are the warrior-saints, men who have fought for Church and Empire and now enjoy divine illumination. Like the ruler-saints found in the next heaven, that of Jupiter, they were all men of action. What sets these spirits of Mercury and Jupiter apart from those of Mars is the absence of any flaws in their character. Justinian, and the others in the sphere of Mars, sought honor and glory. As the rays of their love for God were less lively in their ascent to Him, so the illumination he bestowed upon them was less full in its intensity. The souls in Mercury and Jupiter are also men of action, but their service of God was unmarred by earthly ambitions; hence they enjoy a greater measure of illumination than their less exalted comrades. Here Dante is telling us that in this life greater spiritual illumination is granted to those saints who, living a life of action, are unflawed in their character.

In Mercury Dante-Pilgrim meets his great-great grandfather, Cacciaguida, a knight of the Empire who met his death as a crusader, and "came from martyrdom to this peace."[47] Cacciaguida contrasts the corruption of contemporary Florence with its simplicity and

----------

45. _Paradiso_ XIII, 94-102.

46. See Gilson, _Dante the Philosopher_, pp. 256-276, 140-141.

47. _Paradiso_ XV, 148.

93

uprightness in his own time. He condemns his com-
patriots' decline in virtue. Florentines are now
preoccupied with money-making and extravagant display.
The city that once brought forth hardy, dutiful men,
and women free from paint and pretensions, now begets
slaves of cupidity. By drawing this idealized portrait
of an earlier Florence[48] Dante-Author dramatically
highlights the disordered condition of Florence in his
day.

The cause of this disorder has been the swelling
of Florence's population by the addition of new
arrivals from the surrounding country. "The mixture of
peoples was ever the beginning of the city's ills,"
Cacciaguida asserts.[49]   As Richard Kay says, "Florence
is dysfunctional because it has more persons than one
community can absorb; its excessive size exaggerates
its faults...; sheer numbers are no substitute for
quality and efficiency."[50]   Old leading families have
disappeared or have been by corrupted by the meanness
of spirit, lust for profits, and greed for undeserved
honors that have come to characterize Florence. With
the advantage of hindsight, Eric Auerbach attributes
Dante's disgust with Florence to the city's rising
bourgeois, secular, post-medieval spirit. Dante, writing in the midst of the changes that were taking place,
did not see matters so clearly.   But bearing this in
mind, Auerbach's description is worth repeating.

> Florence of all the Italian towns offered the
> clearest example of what Dante could not but
> regard as absolute evil.  For it was here
> that the new commercial, middle class spirit
> first flowered and achieved self-awareness;
> it was here that the great metaphysical
> foundations of the political world were
> first, in a consistently pragmatic spirit,
> evaluated and exploited for purely political
> ends; it was here that every earthly insti-
> tution, regardless of its transcendent origin
> and authority, came to be considered, with
> cold calculation, as a counter in a game of

----------

48. See Vossler, _Medieval Culture_, Vol. II, p. 12.

49. _Paradiso_ XVI, 67-68.

50. _Dante's Swift and Strong_, p. 200.

forces--an attitude which became prevalent in
every section of the population. And despite
many setbacks that way of thinking brought
Florence success even in Dante's time.

Dante wanted none of it. He would
never have recognized a political life based
on autonomous earthly success; the earthly
world lies in the hands of God; only those
who draw legitimacy from God are entitled
to possess its goods, and then only to the
extent provided for by the legitimation. A
struggle for earthly goods is a trespass
against the divine will; it signifies
anti-Christian confusion, and even on the
practical plane it can lead only to disaster,
to secular and eternal ruin.[51]

Canto XVIII sees Dante and Beatrice ascend from
Mars to Jupiter. The effect of Jupiter's light is to
infuse justice into man's character. The souls Dante
finds here are those of just rulers. These many
lustrous souls arrange themselves to spell out the
injunction DILIGITE IUSTITIAM QUI IUDICATIS TERRAM
(love justice you that judge the earth). Unlike the
other letters of this sentence, the 'M' at the end of
TERRAM does not then dissolve. It retains its shape
and the other resplendent souls surmount it, forming
first a lily and then the head and neck of an eagle.
This enduring M of TERRAM stands for Monarchy. For
Dante the universal monarchy, the Empire, was the
institution responsible for securing earthly justice.
The M's first being surmounted by a lily (the symbol of
both France and Florence) which merges into the head
and neck of an eagle, is, E. G. Gardner points out, "an
allegory of how the Guelphic powers must submit to the
Empire and form peacefully an integral part of this
complete universal monarchy."[52] The design of the M
surmounted by the eagle is explicitly declared to be
the design of God.[53] This is Dante-Author's way of
re-asserting once again the divine origin and authority

----------

51. Dante, Poet of the Secular World, pp. 124-126.

52. Dante's Ten Heavens: A Study of the Paradiso (New
York: Scribner's, 1900), p. 133.

53. Paradiso XVIII, 109-111.

of the Empire. Earthly justice is the effect of heavenly[54] justice, "our justice is the effect of ... heaven".[54] This is true both for political and individual life. In the political realm, the divinely ordained Empire is the dispenser of earthly justice. For the individual, justice is a virtue toward which the soul is disposed by the effect of the planet Jupiter. As Charles Martel explained in Canto VIII, the influence of the stars on men's characters is ultimately the influence of God. Justice, both in individual men and women and in the political world, is of divine origin.

This assertion that the Empire is God's chosen instrument to bring about earthly justice is immediately followed by Dante-Author's invocation of God's wrath upon those churchmen whose avarice leads to the obscuring of Jupiter's beams, to the frustration of God's design for earthly justice.[55] The virtual apostasy of the Church's leaders, an apostasy proclaimed not in their words but in their deeds, is again declared to be the chief cause of the world's ills.

In the following canto the eagle speaks. Made up of the spirits of many rulers, it nonetheless speaks with one voice saying "I and mine when its meaning was we and ours."[56] It thereby expresses the divinely ordained harmony of just rulers within the Empire. But in Dante's day earthly rulers and the earthly Empire knew no such harmony. As the preceding canto ended by decrying the corruption of ecclesiastics, this one ends with the Eagle of Jupiter, the ideal empire, passing its contemptuous judgment on the unjust secular rulers of the age. The severity of this judgment is heightened when we recall that the Paradiso is also about life in this world. The Eagle of Jupiter is no abstract ideal but something that can as much be achieved here in this world as spiritual illumination can be enjoyed here in this life. Consequently, the unjust rulers whom this canto condemns cannot, according to Dante, claim that the nature of the political world compels them to be less just than they would wish to be. Rather, the political world is as disordered as it is

----------

54. Paradiso XVIII, 116-117.

55. Paradiso XVIII, 118-136.

56. Paradiso XIX, 11-12.

in part because its rulers are as unjust as they are. If faithless churchmen must bear prime responsibility for the world's ills, unjust rulers must share the burden with them.

Even the just rulers encountered in the sphere of Jupiter can, however, contribute to the world's disorder. Dante-Author honors one such light, the Emperor Constantine, but at the same time he laments Constantine's well-intentioned attempt to donate temporal authority in the West to the Popes. The Donation provided a pretext for the Church's attempts to usurp the jurisdiction of the Empire. It thereby brought hardship to the world, but did not harm Constantine spiritually.[57] Instead, he ranks among the highly illumined spirits Dante meets in the sphere of Jupiter. He receives such illumination not because good always derived from his deeds, but because he loved justice. The fact that he was fallible in earthly affairs does not preclude Constantine from enjoying spiritual illumination. God does not ask infallibility of His earthly rulers, He asks them to love justice. The results of a particular action are what they are in part because of the response of others to that action; consequently the fact that evil derives from an action does not necessarily condemn its author. In the case of the Donation of Constantine, had the Popes remained true to their own commission, they could never have accepted the Donation. So Dante argues in Monarchy.[58] The evil deriving from the Donation is thus as much or more the responsibility of the Popes than of the Emperor Constantine.

To fulfill their parts in God's plan it is enough that earthly rulers love justice. But if others, such as leading churchmen, fail to perform their parts, the world can still go astray. The Empire, acting by itself, cannot ensure the right order of the world. It requires both Empire and Church to perform this task. Here the Comedy differs from Monarchy. Monarchy argues that in principle the Empire by itself is capable of bringing man to earthly felicity in a peaceful, ordered, temporal realm. The Comedy's position is that since the advent of Christianity at least, this is not true. The capacity of the Church to influence this

----------

57. Paradiso XX, 58-60.

58. Book III, Ch. 10.

97

world, either for good or for ill, is so great that its
proper functioning is essential if right order is to be
enjoyed on earth.

From Jupiter Beatrice and Dante ascend to the
sphere of Saturn. Here Dante meets the illustrious
spirits of great contemplatives. He is greeted by the
soul of Saint Peter Damian, monk, ascetic, and critic
of laxity amongst churchmen. Peter Damian caustically
contrasts the poverty and simplicity of the early
leaders of the Church with the self-indulgent, over-
stuffed, modern Church leaders, surrounded by servants
to prop them up and lift their trains. At this
description, the souls in the still, contemplative
silence of this heaven "raised a cry of such volume
that nothing here on earth could be likened to it;
nor did I understand it, its thunder so overcame
me."[59] Dante-Pilgrim turns to Beatrice like a child
running to its mother. Beatrice, "like a mother who
quickly comforts her pale and breathless boy with the
voice that has often reassured him,"[60] explains that
this terrifying thunderclap is actually the prayer of
the contemplatives. In their righteous zeal they are
outraged by the appalling spectacle presented by the
corrupt earthly ecclesiastics. These divinely illumined contemplatives are neither blind to the world's
affairs nor indifferent to them. Instead, attuned as
they are to the mind of God, they share His wrath at
such consequential wrongdoing.[61] After hearing this
explanation from Beatrice, Dante meets the soul of
Saint Benedict. The founder of the Benedictine order
denounces the avarice, pride, self-indulgence, and
neglect of prayer of contemporary monks. "The walls
that were once an abbey have become dens, and the cowls
worn by the monks are sacks full of rotten
meal."[62] Saint Peter Damian has criticized the
corruption of the active clergy. Saint Benedict does
the same for the contemplative orders of the Church.
Between them, these two saints pronounce stern judgment
on both the Church's aspects.

----------

59. Paradiso XXI, 140-142.

60. Paradiso XXII, 4-6.

61. See Sinclair, Paradiso, p. 327.

62. Paradiso XXII, 76-78.

Dante-Author's denunciation of the Church continues to build in intensity in these cantos. It will reach its climax in Canto XXVII, where he will have Saint Peter, the first Pontiff, say of the man who was Pope in 1300, the year in which the Comedy is set: "He that usurps on earth my place, my place, my place, which in the sight of the Son of God is empty, has made of my tomb a sewer of blood and filth, so that the apostate who fell from here above Satan takes comfort there below."[63] Only in this stomach-turning imagery does Dante-Author convey the full force of his disgust with the corruptions of the earthly Church.

Beatrice and Dante now ascend completely beyond the planets. They rise to the eighth heaven, the sphere of the fixed stars. To appreciate the higher heavens which he is entering, Dante "must have eyes clear and keen" Beatrice tells him.[64] Beatrice's concern is not with his physical eyes, but with the eye of his soul, his spiritual awareness. To sharpen his spiritual perceptiveness Beatrice commands him to look at the universe from his vantage point in the stars. By looking towards the place from whence he has come, Dante-Pilgrim gains a better appreciation of where he now is. From this perspective the earth and its affairs appear greatly diminished in importance.

With my sight I returned through every one of
the seven spheres [Saturn, Jupiter, Mars,
Sun, Venus, Mercury and Moon], and I saw this
globe [the Earth] such that I smiled at its
paltry semblance; and that judgment which
holds it for least I approve as best, and he
whose thought is on other things may rightly
be called just.... The little threshing-
floor that makes us so fierce all appeared to
me from hills to river mouths, while I was
wheeling with [the constellation of] the
eternal Twins.[65]

Dante-Pilgrim clearly sees the absolute superiority of the Supreme Good to paltry secondary goods. The earthly concerns, both public and private, which so

----------

63. Paradiso XXVII, 22-27.

64. Paradiso XXII, 125-126.

65. Paradiso XXII, 133-138, 151-153.

deeply matter to most men, can seem mere trifles when seen from the perspective of a greatly illumined soul.

Edmund Gardner comments that "in a momentary vision, with the capacity of his inward soul enlarged, he looks down upon the whole Universe, and estimates aright the relative values of all things in heaven and earth."[66] Natalino Sapengo suggests that in the years when he was writing the Comedy, Dante went from intense concern for the world, through a lessened concern, to, in the Paradiso, "a growing detachment". As his detachment grew, so grew his rejection of the world. "With this growing detachment come pages in the Paradiso where Dante contemplates from on high this little globe, this wretched earth that is a nothingness compared to celestial reality and yet is so bloodied by human strife, 'the threshing floor that makes us so ruthless'."[67]

This striking devaluation of earthly affairs, including political affairs, is spoken not by Dante-Author but by Dante-Pilgrim, whose spiritual illumination by now is great but not complete. Both Sapengo and Gardner believe that these words represent the view of Dante-Author, but it is clear from the movement of the poem as a whole that Dante-Pilgrim's lucidity of spiritual consciousness increases as the poem goes on. Since the culmination of Dante-Pilgrim's journey has not yet been reached, these words cannot constitute Dante-Author's mature vision. Instead, they convey how earthly affairs can look to an elevated but still growing spiritual consciousness. From such an elevated perspective earthly affairs can indeed seem paltry.

There is detachment from earthly affairs in the Paradiso. But this detachment is that of Dante-Pilgrim, not Dante-Author. There is no detachment in the words Dante-Author addresses directly to the reader at the beginning of Canto XI: "O INSENSATE care of mortals, how vain are the reasonings that make thee beat thy wings in downward flight!" Nor is detachment evident in the speech Dante-Author puts in the mouth of Saint Peter in Canto XXVII, ("he that usurps on earth my place, my place, my place, which in the sight of

----------

66. Dante's Ten Heavens, p. 168.

67. "How the Commedia Was Born," pp. 14-16.

the Son of God is empty, has made of my tomb a sewer of
blood and filth...." etc). Since the characters Dante-
Pilgrim meets in Paradise are in the immediate presence
of God (as Dante-Pilgrim as yet is not), they speak the
truth; their words express the views of Dante-Author.
Thus Saint Peter's denunciation represents Dante's own
views. Dante-Author remains passionately concerned
with earthly matters throughout the Paradiso. As
Umberto Cosmo remarks, Dante-Author's "poetical inspiration was to a large extent derived from his strong
political feelings." Although the spiritual vision of
the Paradiso greatly transcends earthly politics, "it
did not distract his attention from politics. Indeed,
the latter was a source of inspiration for his
poetry."[68]

It is Dante-Pilgrim, not Dante-Author who experiences detachment from earthly affairs. Dante-Pilgrim
is traversing a new realm of spiritual illumination.
It takes him time to grow into this illumination and to
integrate his knowledge of earthly affairs into his
expanded spiritual consciousness.

We should note that Dante-Pilgrim's attitude
toward the world in this canto is one of detachment,
not rejection. Despite its paltry semblance, its
unworthiness to be the chief and frequently the sole
focus of men's thoughts and desires, despite the
capacity of this little threshing-floor to goad men's
fierceness, Dante-Pilgrim does not denounce it or rail
against it; instead he smiles at it. He states his
judgment dispassionately, like one so caught up in the
light of the Supreme Good that all lesser goods pale by
comparison.

Dante-Pilgrim's present evaluation of the earth is
colored by the novel experience of viewing it from the
perspective of the eternal, from the constellation of
"the eternal Twins." His claim to see from a vantage
point in eternity is not a strong one. While figur-
atively speaking he describes the position from which
he looks as being eternal, literally he is only in the
sphere of the fixed stars. This suggests that here he
has but an inkling of eternity. He certainly does not
have the depth of acquaintance with it that he will
subsequently acquire. Nevertheless, temporal earthly
affairs can look infinitesimally petty seen against the

----------

68. Handbook, p. 123.

backdrop of a glimpse of eternity. Eternity transcends time. Even the longest, most consequence-filled span of time is but a snap of the fingers in its realm, the entire earth but a grain of sand. Looking at the world from the standpoint of eternity is one possibility for human consciousness, and its rarity and power make it precious. Nevertheless, it is incomplete. Time and eternity interpenetrate, and to see the world solely from the point of view of either is to miss the fullness of the Whole. God and the illumined saints of Heaven see the world in both time and eternity. These more experienced inhabitants of eternity know detachment, but they feel intense commitment as well. Just as eternity permeates time, so does commitment go hand in hand with their detachment. This was seen in the heaven of Saturn, where Dante-Pilgrim met the souls of illumined contemplatives. For all their silence and detachment, they rent the air with a thunderous shout when Saint Peter Damian described the corruptions of earthly churchmen. For these souls, contemplative detachment and intense concern for earthly affairs are not contradictory, but integral parts of a greater Whole. Dante-Pilgrim has not yet risen to their level. He has yet to integrate time and eternity, multiplicity and unity, commitment, and detachment, in his vision. This he will do only when he reaches the Empyrean, when he will enter the immediate presence of God. As yet he is still a pilgrim in need of tutelage. The perception of the earth's inconsequence belongs to Dante-Pilgrim rather than Dante-Author.

Sinclair points out that Dante-Pilgrim's spiritual progress in Paradise is not linear but rather tacks back and forth. Dante repeatedly gets absorbed in something, usually Beatrice, following which he directs his attention outward to the living landscape that surrounds him.[69] When Dante is oriented toward Beatrice his inward, spiritual perceptiveness grows, usually symbolized by his rising to a higher sphere of Heaven. After having been caught up in the wonder of this inward spiritual revelation, he is ready to look outward and incorporate what he sees there into his now heightened awareness. Dante-Author is telling us that the process of spiritual illumination proceeds by two steps that are repeated again and again. The first consists of inward spiritual growth, the second of re-evaluating

----------

69. Paradiso, pp. 341-342. See also Stambler, Dante's Other World, p. 79.

external reality in light of the new illumination. Neither Dante-Pilgrim's absorption in spiritual illumination nor his consequent heightened understanding of the external world should be taken as Dante-Author's picture of the Whole. Both represent phases on the soul's journey toward discerning the Whole.

The passage in Canto XXII where Dante-Pilgrim looks down from the "eternal Twins" on the "paltry semblance" of the earth is part of this pattern. These words are spoken by Dante-Pilgrim following his ascent from Saturn to the sphere of the fixed stars. As usual, this ascent has been made by the power of Beatrice (grace, revelation). Having experienced the internal illumination symbolized by the ascent to the constellation of "the eternal Twins" in the heaven of the fixed stars, Dante-Pilgrim now looks back at the external universe. Against the background of his first glimpse of eternity the earth by comparison looks inconsequential. But his familiarity with eternity will increase, and his capacity to comprehend the interpenetration of time and eternity, and to integrate concern with detachment, will grow. The world will not always look inconsequential to Dante-Pilgrim.

In the heaven of the fixed stars Dante-Pilgrim meets, among others, Saint Peter, the first Pope. Peter examines Dante on his faith. Dante-Pilgrim passes this examination splendidly. He concludes his reply to Saint Peter's questions with the words "thou didst enter the field poor and fasting to sow the good plant that was once a vine [the Church] and now becomes a thorn."[70] These words, so critical of the contemporary Church, meet with Peter's approval. Later, at the end of Dante's stay in this sphere, Peter himself savagely rebukes the Church, and especially its Popes, for the depths to which it has fallen. It is here that Peter savagely denounces Boniface VIII as "he that usurps on earth my place, my place, my place" and "has made of my tomb a sewer of blood and filth".[71] Peter declares that the Church was established and nurtured by its early martyr Popes not to be used for gain of gold, but for gain of the happy life of spiritual beatitude. It was not the intention of the early Popes that the Church should be a political force, taking sides in

----------

70. Paradiso XXIV, 109-111.

71. Paradiso XXVII, 22-27.

103

secular political controversies and making war on the baptized. Nor did they intend that the Papacy should become a peddler of "sold and lying favors", indulgences and other Papal dispensations granted in return for money. Indeed, says Peter, "ravening wolves in shepherd's clothing are seen from here above through all the pastures." He concludes his appraisal of the existing Church with the words: "O fair beginning, to what base end art thou to fall!"[72] Peter's speech is Dante-Author's own cri de coeur for the Church whose mission he so prized and whose degeneracy he so feelingly deplored.

Despite the horrifying extent of the earthly Church's depravity, Dante-Author does not despair for it. Saint Peter foresees God acting to rescue the Church from its sad condition, just as in the past He acted through the Roman general Scipio to save the Empire from the mortal threat of Hannibal's Carthaginians.[73] Again Dante-Author treats Church and Empire as parallel public institutions, institutions ordained by God and under His care. Dante's doctrine of the Empire's coordinate status with the Church is affirmed, and the Comedy's focus on both great public institutions is maintained.

Dante-Pilgrim next rises with Beatrice to the Empyrean. Compared to the illumination he will here receive, all previous revelations pale by comparison. This final illumination takes longest to achieve and has many stages to it. On entering the Empyrean, Dante is dazzled by the intensity of its light. He comes through this experience with his spiritual awareness heightened. His spiritual eyes now strengthened, he can at last bear any intensity of light. Yet still his spiritual consciousness is far from being focused with perfect clarity, for he cannot yet adequately comprehend the fullness of the Empyrean. Beatrice instructs him to drink of the water of the river of light that flows from God. As soon as he touches his eyelids to these waters, his spiritual vision takes another leap forward. The river of lights "seemed to me to have become round."[74] Dante-Pilgrim has passed from time,

----------

72. Paradiso XXVII, 40-60.

73. Paradiso XXVII, 61-63.

74. Paradiso XXX, 89-90.

104

symbolized by the linear direction of a river, to eternity, symbolized by a circle.[75] With his entry into eternity the first phase of this, Dante-Pilgrim's final illumination, concludes.

Now and only now is Dante-Pilgrim prepared to see earthly affairs in their true light. As if to demonstrate that temporal earthly affairs are indeed part of eternity, and that the souls who dwell there are still concerned with earthly affairs, Beatrice, herself an inhabitant of the Empyrean, points out to Dante the throne prepared in Heaven for the Emperor Henry VII. Beatrice's subsequent words express Dante-Author's own continued commitment to the Empire and its faithful heads whose representative here is Henry. Supposedly speaking in 1300, Beatrice explains that Henry's coming expedition to restore the rule of the Empire in Italy will be thwarted by the cupidity of men and the perfidy of the Church's head.[76] In her final words in the poem, Beatrice foretells how that perfidious Pope (Clement V) shall be thrust head down by God into the flaming agony of Hell. Beatrice's words are the last explicit discussion of earthly affairs in the Comedy. Coming as they do in the Empyrean, in God's immediate presence, from one who speaks for Dante-Author with an authority possessed by no other character in the poem, they constitute a dramatic reiteration of the importance of earthly affairs, of the idea that both Empire and Church are required for the right-ordering of the world, and of Dante's charge that the "mundane greed" of the Church's leaders is the cause of the world's going awry.

Dante-Author treats political matters at the beginning of Dante-Pilgrim's experience of the Empyrean. This suggests that of the subjects discussed here, this one, in his judgment, is the least important. Political affairs are less important than, and come before, the more important Beatific Vision, which occurs at the end of Dante-Pilgrim's stay in the Empyrean, at the very end of the poem. But the fact that political affairs are found in the Empyrean, and that they are discussed with feeling by Beatrice, indicates that for Dante-Author political matters have an importance that is not

----------

75. Singleton, Divine Comedy, Paradiso, 2 Commentary, p. 499.

76. Paradiso XXX, 133-148.

105

eclipsed even in the highest heaven. Earthly political matters cannot disturb the perfect order of Heaven. Accordingly there is detachment in Heaven from earthly affairs. But since temporal political matters are a part of the greater Whole of God's Realm, they are also matters of concern for God, for his saints, and for Dante.

Dante is amazed by the Empyrean. "I, who had come to the divine from the human, to the eternal from time, and from Florence to a people just and sane, with what amazement must I have been filled!"[77] This passage contains Dante-Author's ultimate censure of Florence, the city that had exiled him, the city that was a leader of the Guelf cause in Italy and had done so much to oppose the mission of the Emperor Henry to Italy, the city whose unbridled greed and self-assertiveness symbolized for him all that was wrong with contemporary Italy. Florence is as far from being a people just and sane as the temporal is from the eternal and the human from the divine. But while this may seem an unbridgeable gulf to one lost in the dark wood of the soul's disorder, in fact it is not. Dante-Pilgrim has learned that time exists within eternity, and that man can rise from the human to the divine. Accordingly, earthly disorder can be transformed so that earthly affairs reflect the order and justice of God's universe. Earthly men can rise from being slaves to cupidity to become just and sane. In his ascent Dante-Pilgrim has had the guidance of Virgil (classical virtue and learning) and Beatrice (grace and revelation). Others can avail themselves of the same helpers. In principle, Florence need not forever be far removed from being a people just and sane. At the time that Dante writes, however, the corruption of the Church and the weakness of the Empire have made of Florence and the rest of the world below the hunting ground of the three beasts of the prologue to the Inferno.

Beatrice ascends to her place in the court of Heaven, and Saint Bernard appears to guide Dante-Pilgrim on his last steps. Saint Bernard symbolizes mystical contemplation. Bernard turns Dante's eyes upward to the Holy Virgin Mary. Dante's aspiring gaze

----------

77. Paradiso XXXI, 37-40.

leads him to clearer understanding. Mary, he sees, is "the Queen of Heaven", "the Empress"[78] and around her are gathered the leading dignitaries of this realm. Heaven is God's eternal Empire, the great evangelists and apostles His nobles. In Canto XXV Saint James said to Dante-Pilgrim: "Our Emperor [God], of His grace, wills that thou shouldst come before thy death face to face with His nobles in the inner chamber, so that [thou shouldst see] the truth of this court".[79] The image of Heaven as the court of God was first suggested in Canto II of the _Inferno_. There Virgil told Dante-Pilgrim how Saint Lucy commended Dante in his plight to Beatrice, and how Beatrice descended from Heaven to direct Virgil to Dante's aid. The _Paradiso_ confirms and elaborates this picture of Heaven as an imperial court. The political significance of this depiction of Heaven is that it powerfully buttresses Dante's idea of universal monarchy. N. E. E. Swan perceptively notes that Dante-Author "transfers the Empire to Heaven, seeking a sanction for the earthly institution by representing it as a reflection of the political order (so to say) of the celestial world."[80]

Saint Bernard prays that Mary intercede for Dante-Pilgrim, that he may receive the ultimate illumination, the Beatific Vision. She grants this request, and "from that moment" Dante says, "my vision was greater than our speech, which fails at such a sight, and memory too fails at such excess."[81] Reaching with his gaze "the Infinite Goodness", "the Eternal Light" he sees the form of God's plan for His entire universe, the divine order which God wills for all His creatures. Deep in the mind of God, love binds together the scattered elements of creation.[82] Dante sees "the absolute principle of this union, this 'conflation' or fusion of all things temporal and eternal in the Creator."[83]

----------

78. _Paradiso_ XXXI, 100; XXXII, 119.

79. _Paradiso_ XXV, 40-44.

80. "The Politics of Dante's Divina Commedia," _Church Quarterly Review_, CV (1927), 51.

81. _Paradiso_ XXXIII, 55-57.

82. _Paradiso_ XXXIII, 86-90.

83. Singleton, _Paradiso_, _2 Commentary_, p. 579.

Dante-Author does not claim to be able to recall this vision in any detail.[84] Quite the contrary. "My vision almost wholly fades"[84] he writes. Now, in his role as poet, he has to ask God to grant him again "a little" of what was previously bestowed upon him so that his poem may reveal "but a gleam" of that glory. But to claim to remember even a little of the divine plan is to claim immense authority for Dante-Author. In his letter to Can Grande, Dante heatedly maintains this claim.[85] That letter proclaims the authenticity of the entire final vision, which includes not only the knowledge of the union of all temporal and eternal things in the mind of God, but also the subsequent but politically less relevant direct vision of the Holy Trinity. The Beatific Vision and the poem conclude with Dante's being entirely caught up in God. Both his intellect's desire for vision and his will's striving for union with the desired object are finally satisfied.[86] He is as much at one with his Creator as the sun and stars, which never were estranged from Him. The poem's conclusion is an image of human fulfillment, of being wholly moved by the love of God: "now my desire and will, like a wheel that spins with even motion, were revolved by the Love that moves the sun and the other stars."[87]

Literally, the Paradiso tells of Dante's journey through the successive heavens, culminating in his being granted the Beatific Vision at the end of his stay in the Empyrean. On a deeper level it is the story of the progressive spiritual illumination of the intellect in this life. The heavens he visits are ways of depicting the stages of the soul's awakening. Politically, the Paradiso develops two themes. One is the theme of the fulfillment of the active life. The Purgatorio has already asserted that the active life can reach its full human flowering only when the will has become completely attuned to the will of God. But the active life is capable of being lived not only on

----------

84. Paradiso XXXIII, 61-62.

85. Epistolae, Letter X, para. 28, pp. 208-209.

86. Singleton, Divine Comedy, Paradiso, 2 Commentary, p. 587.

87. Paradiso XXXIII, 143-145.

the purely human level. Divine grace permits men to transcend the merely natural to enjoy the blessing of supernatural illumination. When persons so blest lead active lives they bring to the life of action a new dimension of fulfillment, a spiritual fulfillment that complements the natural fulfillment they already enjoy. Supernatural illumination enhances the capacities of persons to live and enjoy a life of action. It does not obviate that life.

The second political theme of the _Paradiso_ is a corollary of the first. It concerns the significance of earthly affairs in the light of the eternal. While Dante indicates that at some stages of the soul's journey it may find earthly affairs inconsequential in comparison to the eternal, he does not maintain that this is a true valuation of the significance of earthly matters. On the contrary, the _Paradiso_ repeatedly suggests that concern for earthly affairs does not disappear when spiritual illumination comes. In the Empyrean itself, the part of Heaven that is symbolic of the highest state of consciousness, earthly matters have their place. Temporal affairs are part of the eternal Whole. While the immensity of eternity breeds a detachment from earthly matters that seems strange to most inhabitants of "this little threshing-floor that makes us so fierce", earthly affairs are very much a part of God's universe. They are, consequently, matters of concern for spiritually illumined men and women. Even illumined souls who lead contemplative lives, away from the hurly-burly of activity, are deeply concerned by the ills of the political world. The cause of these ills remains in the _Paradiso_ what it was in the _Purgatorio_; the cupidity of the Church. By weakening the Empire, and by neglecting its own true vocation, the voracious Church denies men the guidance they need to set their individual and collective lives in order.

## Chapter 6

## THE PATTERN OF THE COMEDY'S POLITICAL IDEAS

There is a pattern to the political ideas of The Divine Comedy. An internal logic integrates its key political concepts into a coherent whole. By identifying that pattern, this chapter will bring the Comedy's political thought into sharp focus.

Four major concerns characterize the Comedy's political thinking. First, it considers the nature and ends of man. Man is both a natural and a spiritual creature. He has a temporal and an eternal end, and can enjoy both natural and spiritual felicity. Success or failure in achieving these ends and their attendant happiness depends on whether his loves direct him toward goods that have the capacity to satisfy his deepest longings or toward goods that cannot do so. Second, the Comedy considers the public institutions that should aid man in attaining his ends. Church and Empire have the functions of directing man toward the higher goods, those which lead to the attainment of his ends and the enjoyment of felicity. Third, the Comedy considers the disordered condition of the political world, and what needs to be done to set it right. The problems of the world stem from the failure of its public institutions, the Church and the Empire, to perform their proper tasks. For the world to be properly ordered, these institutions must return to the faithful performance of their duties. Finally, The Divine Comedy considers the significance of political matters in the light of the greater Whole. These four themes shape the pattern of The Divine Comedy's political ideas.

### The Nature and Ends of Man

Five important ideas figure prominently in the Comedy's conception of the nature and ends of man. The distinctive nature of man is the first. The second is the doctrine of man's two ends and the happiness that attends on each. The relationship between these ends is the third idea. Next comes Dante's understanding of the process by which men seek to attain felicity, his theory of love. The psychological conditions under which happiness can be achieved is the fifth idea.

**The Nature of Man.**  Man is a unique being for Dante. Of all creatures man alone was created to combine in his nature both life's spiritual and temporal aspects. This is an important feature of Dante's political thinking.  From it he fashions a novel argument for excluding the Popes and the Church from the exercise of political power.

**Man's Two Ends.**  The idea that man's nature contains opposite qualities (temporal and eternal, natural and spiritual) leads to the assertion that man has two ends, one corresponding to each aspect of his nature. The Garden of Eden depicts man's natural, temporal end.  Here he enjoys the happiness of exercising his natural powers to the full, as God created him to exercise them.  As Eden symbolizes man's temporal end, Heaven symbolizes his eternal end.  In addition to enjoying the perfection of their natural capacities, men and women may be enabled by God's grace to experience spiritual illumination.  Living in the awareness of the eternal, joyfully participating in the peace and order that emanates from creation's Source, the spiritually illumined unceasingly enjoy being in the direct presence of "the Eternal Light", "the Infinite Goodness".[1]  This "passing beyond humanity"[2] is man's fulfillment as a spiritual creature, his eternal end.

As for the means by which man attains his ends, the Comedy holds that to reach either of his ends, fallen man must acquire both the moral and intellectual, and the spiritual virtues.  The attainment of even man's temporal end depends upon the possession of some spiritual virtue.  To reach Eden, souls must possess faith; without it they are denied entrance to the mountain of Purgatory upon which Eden rests.  Similarly, the enjoyment of man's spiritual end requires the possession of the moral and intellectual virtues; only those who have first experienced the fulfillment of their purely natural capacities in Eden can rise to the spiritual illumination symbolized by Heaven.  In the Comedy both moral and spiritual virtues are needed for man to enjoy either temporal or eternal felicity. These ends cannot be reached independently; they are experienced in the course of the same process, the pilgrimage of the soul toward God.

----------

1. Paradiso XXXIII, 81-83.

2. Paradiso I, 70.

**The Relation of Man's Two Ends.** Unlike the <u>Monarchy</u>, the <u>Comedy</u> does not flatly describe man's two ends as "duo ultima", two ultimate ends. Yet it does see them as separate; each in its own way completes one aspect of man's nature. This is the import of the two suns imagery of Purgatorio XVI. According to Etienne Gilson, "the distinction between the road of the world and the road of God, each lightened by its own sun, is a faithful reflection of the distinction between the two final goals to which the Pope and Emperor lead humanity in the Monarchy."[3]

The relation between man's ends is not a simple one, however. The heavens rise above the mountain top of Eden, which might be thought to symbolize the superiority of man's spiritual end to his natural end. This may be the case, but it does not preclude man's natural end from being a goal in an of itself, independent of his eternal end. To draw an analogy from the political realm, if states can be sovereign and independent entities despite differences in prestige, power, size, and wealth, man's two goals can each be an end in itself, despite their being unequal in dignity.

The fundamental thrust of Dante's two final ends position is to foreclose the argument that since man's eternal goal is his sole ultimate goal, the Church, which has charge of it, must have authority over the Empire, which has charge of what is only an intermediate goal, the goal of temporal felicity. Dante therefore tries to establish that man's temporal end is not just a means to his eternal end, but is an end in itself. It is the complete fulfillment of man's powers as a natural creature, and is in this sense ultimate. But God, through his power, can raise man to the enjoyment of the Beatific Vision, a passing beyond humanity which is more exalted than the enjoyment of temporal felicity. Temporal happiness <u>is</u> a lesser happiness than eternal happiness, but it is still an end in itself, the fulfillment of man <u>qua</u> man. As such it is not of merely instrumental value and does not entail the subordination of the Empire to the Church. Even <u>Monarchy</u>, which uncompromisingly holds to the two ultimate ends position, admits that "in a certain

----------

3. <u>Dante the Philosopher</u>, p. 223.

[unspecified] fashion our temporal happiness is subordinate to our eternal happiness."[4] This limited but
unspecified superiority of man's eternal end compli-
cates Dante's argument, but it does not stop man's
temporal end from being in its own way final, the
fulfillment of one aspect of man's nature.

**Dante's Theory of Love.** The psychological process by
which men attempt to find happiness Dante calls love.
Perception takes from external reality a mental impression which once unfolded in the mind may attract the
mind to the object perceived; this is love. But between perception's taking an impression of the object
to the mind and the mind's inclination toward the
object lies a crucial step, for the mind can incline
either toward the object or away from it. The decision
to incline toward or away is the responsibility of the
judgment, "the faculty which counsels and which ought
to hold the threshold of assent."[5] For men to love
goods that bring felicity, judgment, not appetite, must
govern their choices. Men are responsible for their
use of the faculty of judgment, notwithstanding the
fact that it is sometimes opposed by impulses of temperament resulting from the influence of the stars. Men
can, if necessary, overcome these impulses. Possessed
of free will and an innate desire to know God, they are
responsible for their loves.

**The Conditions for the Attainment of Felicity.** Dante's
theory of love explains the conditions under which one
can attain happiness, and the conditions under which
one will fall short of the mark. For the judgment to
direct one toward goods that lead to felicity it must
know what these goods are and be capable of inclining
one toward them. The Comedy teaches that men love
wrongly because of their ignorance of the proper values
of different goods, and because of the intensity of
their appetites. It proclaims God to be the Prime
Good, the good which the intellect needs to know and
toward which the judgment needs to be able to direct
men. Devoid of the "good of the intellect", the judgment's capacity to discern the Prime Good, life is
misery, symbolized by Hell.[6] If the appetites are not

----------

4. Monarchy III. 15.

5. Purgatorio XVIII, 62-63.

6. Inferno III, 18.

114

tamed, cupidity overpowers man's judgment and defeats his attempts to reach the Prime Good, as seen in Dante-Pilgrim's defeat by the she-wolf in his attempt to climb the delectable mountain in _Inferno_ I.

_Purgatorio_ XVI describes the soul's predicament.

> From His hands who regards it fondly before
> it is, comes forth, like a child that sports,
> tearful and smiling, the little simple soul
> that knows nothing, but moved by a joyful
> maker, turns eagerly to what delights it. At
> first it tastes the savor of a trifling good;
> it is beguiled there and runs after it, if
> guide or curb do not divert its love.

Without guidance, men are apt to devote their lives to the pursuit of power, wealth, fame, and other trifling goods. But with help, they can learn to love rightly. Proper guidance can nurture their capacity to discern the Prime Good, and suitable curbs (in the form of good laws) can help tame their appetites. As appetite's power to overwhelm judgment diminishes, judgment's ability to direct man to the Prime Good increases. Under these conditions men can attain their temporal and eternal ends.

This understanding of the nature and ends of man contains distinct elements of optimism. Dante is aware of man's enslavement to cupidity, his fallen nature, and his estrangement from God. In the _Inferno_, he depicts the nature and the enormity of sin with unsurpassed vividness. But in contrast to thinkers such as Saint Augustine and Martin Luther, who believed that the Fall had deprived men of all capacity to choose God's way, Dante is more hopeful. Man is indeed fallen, but the Atonement of Christ has "made man able to raise himself again".[8] Two of the _Comedy_'s three books are devoted to the theme of the raising up of fallen man. The _Purgatorio_ shows men of faith, in fellowship with one another, being purged of sin and cupidity, having their loves rightly ordered, and growing in moral and intellectual virtue. The _Paradiso_ shows men and women who, through God's grace, have grown in spiritual illumination, until ultimately they

----------

7. _Purgatorio_ XVI, 85-93.

8. _Paradiso_ VII, 79-120.

came to the Beatific Vision. Despite his awareness of human sin and cupidity, Dante does not despair for man.

Dante's understanding of man and his ends is a key element in the pattern of his political thinking. He see man as having two aspects to his nature, and two ends. As a natural creature man has a natural end, and as a spiritual creature he has a spiritual end. Each of these ends has its characteristic happiness. In his theory of love Dante spells out how man attempts to achieve felicity, and why he so often fails. Only when judgment is nurtured, appetite is curbed, and man loves God first and lesser goods second will men attain their ends and enjoy felicity. Dante's understanding of man is the basis for both his analysis of the causes of political disorder, and his vision of a properly order-ed world. His desire to help men achieve their ends, to help them traverse the road from misery to happiness, leads him to put forth his explicitly political ideas.

## The Roles of Empire and Church

To curb his appetites, develop his faculty of judgment, put his loves in order, and achieve his goals, man needs help. To provide this aid is the raison d'être of Empire and Church. The Empire's task is twofold. First, it should free man's judgment to choose true goods. Second, it should encourage the development of moral and intellectual virtue. To carry out its task the Empire must uphold good and well-enforced laws, laws that curb appetite and habituate men to virtuous action. But a man can love rightly only if he has some inkling of the Prime Good. The role of the Church is to kindle his spiritual aspira-tion. Then his free and mature judgment shall indeed choose God as its first and greatest love.

The relation of the Empire to the Church is a major theme of Dante's thought. He does not believe that the superior dignity of man's eternal end neces-sitates the superiority of the Pope to the Emperor in temporal affairs. As Etienne Gilson succinctly points out, "Dante's universe is of such a kind that the hierarchy of dignities among ends never gives rise to any jurisdictional hierarchy within it, but rather to the mutual independence" of its various orders.[9] While Dante sees the political order as a part of the greater Whole, he believes that responsibility for coordinating the parts so that they fit harmoniously within the Whole rests with God and not with any earthly figure. The Pope, therefore, does not have charge of man's eternal end, nor does the Emperor have charge of man's temporal end. Pope and Emperor merely direct men to the means by which these ends are attained. It belongs to God rather than the Pope to ensure that secular rulers promote rather than hinder man's progress toward his ends. Consequently a hierarchy of dignity among ends does not entail a hierarchical relationship between the officers who guide man to these ends.

The Comedy thus holds that Church and Empire should be separate and coordinate authorities. The proper ordering of the world is one in which it has two suns (the Empire and the Church) to illuminate the two ways by which man moves toward his ends. One way is that of the world, the curbing of the appetite through well-enforced laws, and the strengthening of the judgment by the acquisition of the moral and intellectual virtues discovered by philosophy. The other is the way of God, in which the soul aspires first to possess the Christian virtues of faith, hope and charity and ultimately to be granted the divine gift of spiritual illumination. The Empire's sun lights up the way of the world, the Church's sun the way of God. In this two-suns imagery the Comedy vividly and deliberately affirms the separate and coordinate status of Empire and Church. Pope and Emperor are two separate officers, having two different functions, directing men to two distinct (though complementary) ends, by different means. Each officer receives his authority directly from God. Consequently, Pope and Emperor are separate officers of equal status. Each is the supreme earthly figure in performing his particular task.

Dante distinguishes the role of the Empire from that of the Church on the basis of his distinction between man as a natural, temporal being, and man as an eternal, spiritual being. As a temporal creature man is capable of natural virtue, the virtue discovered by philosophy, and it is the function of the Emperor to

----------

9. Dante the Philosopher, p. 141.

use his power to facilitate man's acquisition and exercise of such virtue. As a spiritual being man is
capable of spiritual virtue, of faith, of hope, and of
charity. The Pope should use his paternal standing in
the Christian community to inspire men to exercise this
kind of virtue. In Monarchy Dante distinguishes between relations based on paternal standing on the one[10]
hand and relations based on lordship on the other.
The Pope possesses paternal standing but not political
power. Power is an attribute of lordship, and lordship
belongs to the Emperor.[11] The Comedy makes this distinction implicitly. Its Emperor exercises the powers
of lordship; its Pope is called upon to exercise spiritual leadership and renounce temporal power. Dante's
idea of the twofold nature of man provides new grounds
for restricting the Pope's role to that of providing
spiritual leadership. Dante's conclusion was not new,
but his way of arriving at it was.

Empire and Church exist to help man attain his
temporal and spiritual ends. Man needs their help,
for, beset by cupidity and ignorant of the true goods
of life, he is all too apt to lose his way and never
arrive at his goals. The Empire and Church should
illuminate the two roads to man's ends, the road of
earthly virtue and the road of spiritual aspiration.
By so doing they direct man to his ends and to
felicity.

## The Disordered Condition of the World

The disordered condition of the world is the third
theme of the Comedy's political teaching. Dante recognized that neither the Church nor the Empire of his day
faithfully performed its function. He identified the
corruption of the Church, the eclipse of the power of
the Empire, and the consequent absence of proper
guidance for the world's inhabitants as the immediate
sources of the world's deplorable condition. Dante's
prescription for reestablishing right order in the
world follows logically from this understanding of the
causes of the world's disorder.

----------

10. Monarchy III. 11.

11. See Michael Wilks, The Problem of Sovereignty in
the Later Middle Ages (Cambridge, 1963), pp. 104-105.

To explain the ills of the world, the
points primarily to the corruption of the Church,
condemns leading churchmen chiefly for two things:
for temporal power (whose corollary is the usurpat
of the rightful authority of the Empire) and t
seeking after wealth, the sin of avarice. Wealth and
temporal power are goods which by their nature are
inappropriate for churchmen. The glitter of these
goods has blinded many leading churchmen to the Prime
Good, and to their duty to seek that good themselves
and to inspire others to seek it. Such churchmen do
not direct men toward the theological virtues. The
people, consequently, go astray. The fate of such
faithless church leaders is a harsh one. They go to
Hell, symbolic of misery in this life and the next.
Inferno XIX, for example, depicts simonists, popes who
sold (or purported to sell) spiritual goods for money,
thrust head first into the fissures of the rocks of
Hell, the soles of their feet aflame. "Their simony"
remarks Father Kenelm Foster, "was merely the expression and bringing to light of a radical inversion of
values, a substitution of what the Bride of Christ [the
Church] is for by what she is precisely not for." [12]
This insight is applicable not just to those popes who
were simonists, but to all leading churchmen who in
their greed for wealth and power neglect the spiritual
mission of the Church.

For all his caustic rebukes to the Church, Dante
does not neglect the failings of the Empire. The Roman
Law, the basis for directing man toward the moral
virtues known to philosophy, exists, but the Empire
does not ensure that the law is everywhere upheld.
Neither does it maintain peace amongst lesser political
entities. Consequently it fails to restrain men's
appetites and free their judgments to choose goods that
lead to felicity. The political world accordingly
knows wrong and war instead of justice, peace, and
virtue. No more than the Church does the Empire do
what Dante asks of it.

The Empire's failure has two causes. The greed of
the popes for temporal power is one; their pernicious
meddling in temporal politics subverts the Empire and
facilitates the emergence of excessively powerful and
independent national monarchies such as that of France.

----------

12. "The Canto of the Damned Popes: Inferno XIX," Dante
Studies, LXXIX (1969), 61.

is the greed and injustice of temporal
y dominates them no less than high
kings and emperors, with few excep-
aithfully perform their proper duties.
who, while possessing the Christian
cted to cultivate in themselves and in
he moral virtues, receive their just
lley of the Princes in Ante-Purgatory.
before being allowed to enter Purgatory proper and
begin their progress toward felicity, they must endure
a waiting period outside its gates; the journey from
misery to happiness takes them longer than it might.
As the popes and other high churchmen condemned to Hell
failed to direct men to the theological virtues, these
temporal rulers failed in their assigned task of
directing men to the moral and intellectual virtues.

Dante uses some powerful and vivid images to
convey both the enormity and the cause of the world's
wrongs. At the end of the _Inferno_, in the very core of
Hell, the three-mouthed Satan chews three paramount
sinners, Brutus, Cassius and Judas. The betrayal of
the institutions which ought to guide mankind, by men
whose duty it is to support them, results in man's
going astray. At the end of the _Purgatorio_, in the
Pageant of Revelation, the same story is told in different form. The triumphal car of the Church acquires
the plumage of the eagle, the symbol of temporal
power. A harlot now surmounts the car upon which
Beatrice once rode. The harlot embraces and is dragged
off by a brutish giant, the king of France. This
symbolism indicates that the Church, once led by men
whose lives revealed the glory of God, now is dominated
by corrupt churchmen who in their lust for temporal
gain have turned their backs upon spiritual virtue.
The betrayal of Church and Empire by churchmen and
secular rulers alike is the cause of the deformed
condition of the world.

The disordered condition of the souls of most
earthly leaders accounts for the disordered condition
of the world. To properly guide others from misery to
happiness, they must have their own loves rightly
ordered. When Pope and Emperor are both free from
cupidity, neither will have reason to usurp the power
of the other. When Pope and Emperor are both men of
rightly-ordered love, willing God's will, then each
will have the best of reasons to support and cooperate
with the other. The two great institutions, Church and
Empire, can work in harmony, each in its own way helping man toward his ends. This is the positive vision

implied in the Comedy's understanding of the causes of the world's ills. But it is a vision which will be brought to fruition only through the intervention of divine Providence.

The role of Providence in restoring right order to the world is stated strongly in the Comedy. The day will come when God will place Empire and Church under the leadership of men of rightly-ordered love. In Paradiso XXVII Saint Peter foresees God acting to rescue the Church from its sad condition. Beatrice in that same canto sees God as the origin of the sequence of events which will restore the Empire to its rightful state. This latter event, "so long looked-for shall turn the poops where are the prows [cause a one hundred and eighty degree turn]; and then the fleet shall run on the straight course and good fruits shall follow the flower."[13] The responsibility for the right-ordering of the world as a whole rests with God, and not with any earthly figure. The responsibility of earthly leaders, spiritual as well as temporal, is confined to the faithful discharge of the limited duties entrusted to them. Human action will be necessary for right order to come about on earth, but human action by itself will not bring about a restoration of order. Only when human action coincides with the workings of divine Providence will the world be set right.

**The Significance of Political Life in Light of the Whole**

The Comedy's teaching that divine intervention is necessary for the restoration of right order to the world reflects its holistic, God-centered perspective. This perspective, evident throughout the Comedy, comes to the fore in the Paradiso. The Paradiso attempts to convey the indescribable, the vision of the Whole. The Whole encompasses and pervades everything, all aspects of human endeavor, politics no less than art, commerce, learning or religion. Accordingly, political life is not a realm unto itself--it is part and parcel of a larger order.

The permeation of the secular, temporal domaine of politics by the sacred and the eternal is a key

----------

13. Paradiso XXVII, 139-148. Also see Singleton, Divine Comedy, Paradiso, 2 Commentary p. 445.

teaching of the _Paradiso_. For example, Justinian's speech in _Paradiso_ VI treats Rome's political history as sacred history. The Eagle is "the bird of God", Rome "the most holy standard." Rome's triumphs are God's triumphs, her Empire God's Empire. The Empire, and the political world which it superintends, are divinely ordained parts of the order of the Whole. Even the temperaments of political men derive from a spiritual cause. The stars, whose influence on human character derives ultimately from God, give rise to the diverse natures of different men. And these different qualities are infused into individual men and women in keeping with God's plan.

Even justice, a most politically relevant good, stems from God. On earth it is the function of the Empire to uphold the law, to see that justice is done. But earthly justice is the effect of heavenly justice, "our justice is the effect of ... heaven".[14] In both political and individual life justice is of divine origin. Politically, justice is dispensed by the Empire, which for Dante is authorized by God. Individually, justice is a virtue toward which the soul is disposed by God's design, through the effect of the planet Jupiter. Justice, in the individual as in the political world, is part of the greater order of the Whole.

The _Paradiso_ reveals the place of political affairs within the Whole. Here we find a number of different values being placed on political life. Sometimes there is a detachment from earthly affairs in the _Paradiso_. This detachment is associated with a partial and incomplete appreciation of the eternal Whole. It is Dante-Pilgrim, the soul experiencing the progressive growth of spiritual consciousness, who experiences detachment from earthly affairs. It takes him time to integrate his knowledge of earthly affairs into his expanding spiritual awareness. While he is growing, his detachment does not lead him to reject the temporal world. Rather than denouncing it, he smiles at it.

The _Paradiso_ does teach, however, that against the backdrop of a glimpse of eternity earthly doings can appear trivial. Compared to the grandeur of the eternal, lesser goods look inconsequential. The eternal perspective is one possibility for human consciousness.

----------

14. _Paradiso_ XVIII, 116-117.

The temporal perspective is another. Together, these two viewpoints complement one another. Neither is complete in itself; to appreciate but one of this pair of polar opposites is to miss the fullness of the Whole. Souls with more experience of spiritual illumination see the world in both its dimensions, temporal and eternal. They too know detachment from earthly affairs, but their detachment is complemented with intense commitment. The illumined contemplatives of the heaven of Saturn are fiercely indignant at the negligence and corruption of earthly churchmen. Contemplative detachment and intense concern for earthly affairs form integral parts of the holistic vision of these illumined souls. As eternity permeates time, detachment goes hand in hand with committment.

Dante considers the ultimate significance of political affairs in the Empyrean scene. Beatrice's continued concern for political matters authoritatively indicates their significance in the light of the greater Whole. While they are less important in the final scale of things than the Beatific Vision, the fact that political matters are discussed at all in the Empyrean indicates their great significance to Dante. In the highest state of spiritual illumination, earthly political life is seen to be an important part of the greater Whole.

By locating his vision of political right order against the background of the order of the Whole, Dante gives it a plausibility it would otherwise lack. The Comedy is one of the most convincing visions of order ever produced. Its treatment of Hell, Purgatory, Eden and Heaven is so vivid, so authentic, that it captures our imagination. It convinces us that man's two goals are attainable, and that the pilgrimage from misery to happiness is possible and desirable, despite its difficulties, terrors and setbacks. The vision of the ordered Whole prepares us for Dante's call for cooperation between Church and Empire, for each to be led by men of rightly-ordered love, for each in its own proper way to strive to help man attain his temporal and eternal ends. By setting his vision of earthly order in the context of an overarching harmony, Dante greatly strengthens his case. If we look only at earthly tumult, it is easy to conclude that dissonance is an inevitable part of politics. But if we look first at the fundamental harmony of the Whole, then the turbulence of earthly affairs, while still real and poignant, no longer looks unalterable. Sooner or later earthly affairs may share in the order of the Whole.

Three basic themes structure the political teaching of <u>The Divine Comedy</u>. First, Dante's understanding of the nature and ends of man leads him to call upon Empire and Church to aid man in his efforts to attain his ends and enjoy felicity. Second, Dante points to the failure of these institutions to faithfully perform their duties to account for the miserable state of the world. Finally, he concludes that only when the actions of men coincide with the workings of divine Providence will earthly affairs take their proper place within the harmony of God's universe. Together these themes shape the poem's political ideas into an integrated vision of public life seen in the context of the Whole.

# Chapter 7

## CONCLUSION

The political ideas of <u>The Divine Comedy</u> knit together to form a remarkably coherent body of political thought. Not just a few scattered jottings, they are the political theory of one who was active in public life and pondered it deeply. Dante's political vision is conveyed in a poem of remarkable vividness and convincingness. But a coherent set of political ideas, expressed in powerful words, can still be impractical, unoriginal, and without lasting significance. What, if anything, raises the political ideas of the <u>Comedy</u> above this level?

In terms of practicality, the <u>Comedy</u>'s ideas are in one sense seriously deficient. Historically, the Empire for which Dante had such high hopes was doomed. His political ideas were out of step with the historical trends of the time. Even such a sympathetic scholar as Thomas Bergin remarks that "Dante is not, like Machiavelli, setting down the results of his observations, or if so, only infrequently and tangentially; he is throughout defining an ideal."[1] Bergin says this of <u>Monarchy</u>, but his remark applies equally well to the <u>Comedy</u>'s political ideas.

Even if we ignore the historical decline of the Empire and focus on the <u>Comedy</u>'s political ideas as an attempt to prescribe what should be rather than to describe what is, there are still serious difficulties. How are the tasks of Pope and Emperor to be separated in practice? This is no easy question. However, Dante's proposed delineation of responsibilities between Empire and Church is in some limited respects analogous to the separation of spheres of activity of general and regional governments under a system of dual or classical federalism. Conceivably, modern experience with federalism might shed light on Dante's proposal.

According to K. C. Wheare, "what is necessary for the federal principle is not merely that the general

----------

1. <u>Dante</u> (New York: Orion Press, 1965), p. 181.

government, like the regional governments, should operate directly on the people, but, further, that each government should be limited to its own sphere, and, within that sphere, should be independent of the other."[2] Dante was proposing a system of coordinate institutions rather than governments possessing coercive power, but each was to act directly on the people, and each was to be independent within its own field of activity.

Modern federal systems have found it impossible to keep the spheres of activity of the general and regional governments entirely apart. Could the fields of activity of temporal and spiritual leaders any more be kept separate? The eminent Danteist Edward Moore asserts that "there is no such hard and fast line ... between the two parts of man's nature, or the two spheres of his practice. However distinct in conception, they are inseparable in fact.[3]

The separation of the spheres of activity of Church and Empire indeed poses serious difficulties, especially in a theocentric civilization like that of medieval Europe, yet modern federal states also encounter problems of overlapping spheres. If federal systems can succeed despite such difficulties, might not Pope and Emperor tolerate some overlapping of their spheres of responsibility as well? If so, Dante's proposal of separate but coordinate institutions might indeed be practical.

In terms of Dante's thinking cupidity is the key; as long as men are dominated by their greedy appetites, then conflict, aggression, and struggles for institutional aggrandizement are inevitable. To develop his argument further Dante needs to establish that institutional leaders can be men of rightly-ordered love whose cupidity has been stilled. Dante's optimism about the possibilities of human nature leads him to believe that, in principle, cupidity can be overcome. Appetites can be checked, initially through the power of law, and ultimately through the acquisition of the moral virtues through habituation to virtuous action. Men can come to love God first and lesser goods but second through

----------

2. Federal Government (4th ed.; New York and London, 1964), p. 14.

3. Studies in Dante, II, 20.

their acquisition of the theological virtues of faith, hope, and charity and through their reception of divine grace. Thus, in principle, cupidity can be overcome, and the leaders of Church and Empire can be men whose loves are rightly ordered. Then their prime motive for usurping one another's proper tasks will have ceased to exist, and the possibility of cooperation between them will have been greatly enhanced.

But the overcoming of cupidity will not necessarily result in harmonious relations among institutional leaders. Differences in perspective deriving from different institutional vantage-points might lead Pope and Emperor to see the world differently, to have different concerns, different priorities, and different policies, differences which might bring into conflict even men whose loves are indeed rightly ordered. But this objection need not be decisive. Another argument, one that stems from Dante's conviction that men can love God first and lesser goods second, suggests that a basis for cooperation between these officers can be found in their rightly-ordered love. Here again the analogy with federalism may, within strict limits, prove useful. A federal state is successful when, among other things, its political leaders, possessing a common loyalty to their country, have the will to compromise their regional and institutional differences, that their federation might endure. If Emperor and Pope could both love God first and foremost, then, sharing a common loyalty to God, they too might have the will to respect each other's field of activity and to reconcile the differences that arise between them. In Cantos XI and XII of the _Paradiso_ Dante portrays leading representatives of two great orders within the Church as showing just this capacity to overcome the limitations of their institutional vantage-points, illumined as they are by their awareness of being in the direct presence of God.

Notably missing from Dante's treatment of the relations between Empire and Church is any analogue of a supreme court to resolve conflicts about the boundaries of the proper spheres of the two institutions. The _Comedy_ lacks an earthly supreme court (though not a heavenly one). But this absence is not critical. In federal systems what is imperative is not the existence of an institution to define spheres; what is essential is a shared will amongst the leaders to resolve their differences in order to serve their country; it is this will that leads officials of different levels of government to accept and obey the rulings of supreme courts in federal systems. The supreme court is one institutional mechanism for bringing about agreement amongst those who are predisposed to reach agreement. It is not the only such mechanism nor necessarily even the best. Since Dante has shown that the leaders of different institutions can possess the will to reach agreement, the absence of an institutional mechanism to bring it about is not decisive.

In showing that both cupidity and the conflicts that arise from differing institutional loyalties can be overcome, Dante establishes that, in principle, there can be a basis for cooperation and mutual respect between Emperor and Pope. The problem of maintaining harmony between Emperor and Pope is a particular case of an enduring human concern, the problem of bringing concord rather than tumult out of the conflicting impulses of different institutional leaders. The Comedy's answers to this problem, while couched in terms of the institutions and officers of a particular time, are of continuing interest.

But if it is possible for a man to love rightly and be free from cupidity, the question arises, why should not this person have complete authority on earth, temporal as well as spiritual? Why does the mixing of both sorts of authority in one man and one institution necessarily produce ill? William Anderson, in his Dante the Maker, suggests an answer. State and Church are the institutionalization of two tendencies of human nature, each of which has its place in society. One tendency is toward outward activity, the active life. The other is toward inward growth, the contemplative life. State and Church are complementary in that each draws to itself persons who are primarily oriented toward either the outward or the inward life. In a healthy society the two sorts of men "should work in accord acknowledging each other's spheres, and have a yearning and a need for one another...."[4]

The dualism of Church and State reflects "a dualism in human society which has to be brought into balance, otherwise it swings to one of the two extremes that in modern terms Arthur Koestler characterized as those of the Yogi [inward] and the Commissar [outward]." The complete dominance of either State or Church threatens this balance. The State threatens to "take

----------

4. Routledge & Kegan Paul, London, 1980, p. 223.

over and rule all sides of human life, ultimately denying the existence of the spiritual world", as seen in twentieth century totalitarian regimes. This tendency needs to be kept in check. But so does the Church need to be kept in check. The Church is beset by two temptations. On the one hand it is tempted to ignore its spiritual mission and seek power and influence in temporal affairs. When it succumbs, the spiritual dimension of society suffers. On the other hand the Church is tempted to go to the other extreme and retreat from the world as in Dante's day the "Spiritual Franciscans wanted and as many modern proponents of an alternative society desire...." When the Church turns inward upon itself it is diverted from its missionary task. It no longer is vitally engaged in bringing the message of spiritual regeneration to most of the world's people, and again society is the worse. Church and State both need to be restrained from pursuing their perverse tendencies.

If either Church or State is all powerful, it can easily succumb to temptation. But the countervailing authority of the Church can help keep the State in check, by "the spiritual well-being of all its subjects who acknowledge through conscience and faith the existence of a spiritual authority external to the state's control." Similarly, society can constantly recall the Church to its mission to ordinary men and women. The Church needs to be in contact "with a lively and creative population aware that its society's life and creativeness depend on the balance it can achieve between the active life and the contemplative life which must be fostered by the spiritual authority."⁵ For this to happen the Church cannot be all powerful, it cannot dominate society. Society must be sufficiently independent of the Church to call it to the performance of its proper task.

Thus we can see why the joining of temporal and spiritual authority in the same hands is so dangerous; it is destructive of the salutary balance between the institutions that embody the opposite tendencies of human nature. "The one [institution] together with the other must perforce go ill," Dante

----------

5. Anderson, <u>Dante the Maker</u>, p. 223.

writes,[6] "since, joined, the one does not fear the other." The concentration of both functions in one institution necessarily produces ill.

If both Empire and Church are necessary for the well-being of the world, they must be able to cooperate with one another. Dante establishes such a basis for cooperation. The Emperor can help the Church by being receptive to the spiritual teaching of the Church. As Christendom's leading layman, his attentiveness to the spiritual teaching of Pope and Church sets an example for others to follow. This does not, however, give the Pope any right to direct the Emperor in respect to temporal political matters. In Justinian's account of how he heeded the spiritual teaching of Pope Agapetus, he states he took his way beside (not behind) the Church. The Emperor's receptivity to the Pope's spiritual teaching does not detract from his status as an independent power in his own sphere.

The Comedy shows also how popes, by performing their duties as spiritual teachers, can facilitate the work of emperors. On his arrival at the island of Purgatory, Dante-Pilgrim's waist was girded with a reed symbolizing humility. Another reed immediately sprang up in its place. Unlike scarce earthly goods such as power, wealth, and fame, spiritual good is available without limit. When men's attention embraces spiritual goods there is less need for conflict. The Church, by directing men's attention to goods over which they need not quarrel, makes the Empire's task of maintaining order easier. The Comedy thus establishes that there is a practical as well as a theoretical basis for cooperation between Church and Empire.

The political ideas of The Divine Comedy form a logical and sometimes original political theory. Like many medieval thinkers, Dante was not persuaded that the ideal should be abandoned because serious impediments stood in the way of its attainment. This makes him sometimes look naive and unrealistic to modern minds, but his political thought has its redeeming features. Dante showed that, in principle, there can exist a basis for cooperation and mutual respect between different institutional leaders. He showed how the political realm could be part of the order of the Whole and still be independent of the Church. While

----------

6. Purgatorio XVI, 110-112.

the belief that Empire and Church properly have separate fields of activity was far from new, Dante's way of arriving at this conclusion was a novel one. Starting from the idea that man's nature has two aspects, Dante developed new grounds for restricting the Pope's role to that of providing spiritual leadership. This was an original contribution to medieval political thinking.

Dante's greatest achievement, however, is to look beyond the fragmentation of the parts to see how they can fit harmoniously into the greater Whole. By setting his vision of earthly order in the context of the order of the Whole, he makes that vision convincing. He further shows that political life is important in the context of the Whole. Earthly life has real value; man finds his fulfillment as a natural creature in the enjoyment of temporal happiness. Dante thus avoids the world-denying tendencies of medieval Christian thought. At the same time, however, his poetic genius brings home with unparalleled power the medieval vision of man's capacity to enjoy spiritual fulfillment, to rise (through God's grace) to union with the Creator. In fact, it is because Dante preserves the medieval sense of the Whole that he is able to affirm the value of political life so strongly; the public institutions of Empire and Church have vitally important roles to play in helping men and women attain their temporal and eternal ends, in helping human creatures realize the bliss they are born for.

# BIBLIOGRAPHY

## I. Primary Sources

Alighieri, Dante. The Convivio. Translated by P. H.
    Wicksteed. 4th ed. ("Temple Classics Series.")
    London: Dent, 1924.

_____. De Monarchia. The Oxford Text, edited
    by Dr. Edward Moore, with an introduction on the
    political theory of Dante by W. H. V. Reade.
    Oxford: Clarendon Press, 1916.

_____. The Comedy of Dante Alighieri, the
    Florentine. Translated by Dorothy L. Sayers
    and Barbara Reynolds. 3 vols. Harmondsworth,
    Middlesex: Penguin, 1950-1963.

_____. The Divine Comedy. Translated with a
    commentary by John D. Sinclair. 3 vols. New
    York: Oxford University Press, 1965
    (c. 1939-1946).

_____. The Divine Comedy. Translated with a
    commentary by Charles S. Singleton. 6 vols.
    Princeton: Princeton University Press, 1970-1975.

_____. Epistolae: The Letters of Dante.
    Translated by Paget Toynbee. Oxford: Clarendon
    Press, 1966 (c. 1920).

_____. Monarchy and Three Political Letters.
    Translated by Donald Nicholl. London, Weidenfeld
    and Nicholson, 1954.

## II. Secondary Sources:   Books

Anderson, William. Dante the Maker. London: Routledge
    and Kegan Paul, 1980.

Auerbach, Eric. Dante, Poet of the Secular World.
    Translated by Ralph Manheim. Chicago: University
    of Chicago Press, 1961.

133

Barbi, Michele. _The Life of Dante_. Translated by
    Paul Ruggiers. 2nd ed. Berkeley: University of
    California Press, 1954.

Bergin, Thomas G. _Dante's Divine Comedy_. Englewood
    Cliffs, New Jersey: Prentice Hall, 1971.

_____. _Dante_. New York: Orion Press, 1965.

_____. _A Diversity of Dante_. New Brunswick, New
    Jersey: Rutgers University Press, 1969.

Bernardo, Aldo S., and Anthony L. Pellegrini. _A
    Critical Study Guide to Dante's Divine Comedy_.
    Totowa, New Jersey: Littlefield, Adams, 1968.

Brandeis, Irma. _The Ladder of Vision: A Study of
    Dante's Comedy_. Garden City, New York: Doubleday,
    1961.

Chandler, Stanley Bernard, and J. A. Molinaro, (eds.).
    _The World of Dante: Six Studies in Language and
    Thought_. Toronto: University of Toronto Press,
    1966.

Church, Richard William. _Dante, An Essay_. London:
    Macmillan, 1878. First published in the _Christian
    Remembrancer_, January 1850.

Clements, Robert John, (ed.). _American Critical Essays
    on the Divine Comedy_. New York: New York
    University Press, 1967.

Cosmo, Umberto. _A Handbook to Dante Studies_.
    Translated by David Moore. Oxford: Blackwell,
    1950.

Croce, Benedetto. _The Poetry of Dante_. Translated by
    Douglas Ainslie Appel. Mamaroneck, New York:
    Holt, 1971.

Cunningham, Gilbert F. _The Divine Comedy in English:
    a Critical Bibliography_. Edinburgh: Oliver and
    Boyd, 1965-66.

Curtius, Robert. _European Literature and the Latin
    Middle Ages_. Translated by William R. Trask.
    New York: Pantheon, 1953.

Davis, Charles Till. _Dante and the Idea of Rome_.
    Oxford: Clarendon Press, 1957.

D'Entrèves, A. P. Dante as a Political Thinker.
Oxford: Clarendon Press, 1952.

D'Entrèves, A.P. The Medieval Contribution to
Political Thought. New York: Humanities Press,
1959 (c. 1939).

De Sua, William J., and Gino Rizzo, (eds.). A
Dante Symposium in Commemoration of the 700th
Anniversary of the Poet's Birth: 1265-1965.
Chapel Hill: University of North Carolina Press,
1965.

Dunbar, Helen Flanders. Symbolism in Medieval Thought
and its Consumation in the Divine Comedy. New
York: Russell and Russell, 1961.

Fergusson, Francis. Dante. New York: Macmillan, 1966.

Foster, Kenelm. The Mind in Love: Dante's Philosophy.
London: Blackfriars, 1956.

_____. The Two Dantes and Other Studies.
Berkeley: University of California Press, 1978.

Freccero, John, (ed.). Dante: A Collection of Critical
Essays. Englewood Cliffs, New Jersey:
Prentice-Hall, 1965.

Gardner, Edmund G. Dante. London: Dent, 1923.

_____. Dante [a lecture.] Oxford: Oxford
University Press, 1921.

_____. Dante and the Mystics. New York: Octagon,
1968 (c. 1913).

_____. Dante's Ten Heavens: A Study of the
Paradiso. Westminster, New York: Scribner's,
1900.

Gilson, Etienne H. Dante the Philosopher. Translated
by David Moore. London: Sheeds and Ward, 1948.

Grandgent, Charles H. Dante Alighieri. New York:
Ungar, 1966 (c. 1916).

_____. La Divina Commedia di Dante Alighieri.
Rev. ed. Boston: Heath, 1933.

Holmes, George. _Dante_. Oxford: Oxford University
    Press, 1980.

Howell, A. G. F. _Dante: His Life and Work_. London:
    Jack, 1912.

Jones, George Fenwick. _Honor in German Literature_.
    Chapel Hill: University of North Carolina Press,
    1959.

Kantorowicz, Ernst H. _The King's Two Bodies: A Study
    in Medieval Political Theology_. Princeton:
    Princeton University Press, 1957.

Kantorowicz, Ernst H. _Selected Studies_. Locust
    Valley, New York: Augustin, 1965.

Kay, Richard. _Dante's Swift and Strong: Essays on
    Inferno XV_. Lawrence, Kansas: Regents Press of
    Kansas, 1978.

King, Margot and Wesley M. Stevens (eds.). _Saints,
    Scholars and Heroes_. 2 vols. Collegeville,
    Minnesota: St. John's Abbey and University, 1979.

Lenkeith, Nancy. _Dante and the Legend of Rome_.
    London, Warburg Institute, University of London,
    1952.

Lewis, Ewart. _Medieval Political Ideas_. 2 vols.
    London: Routledge and Kegan Paul, 1954.

Mazzeo, Joseph A. _Medieval Cultural Tradition in
    Dante's "Comedy"_. Ithaca, New York: Cornell
    University Press, 1960.

Moore, Edward. _Studies in Dante_. 4 vols. Oxford:
    Clarendon Press, 1896-1917.

Nolan, David, (ed.). _Dante Commentaries_. Dublin:
    Irish Academic Press, 1977.

_____. _Dante Soundings_. Dublin: Irish Academic
    Press, 1981.

Ralphs, Sheila. _Dante's Journey to the Center_. New
    York: Barnes and Noble, 1973.

Reade, William Henry Vincent. _Dante's Vision of
    History_. London: Milford, 1939.

Rolbiecki, John J. The Political Philosophy of Dante
Alighieri. Washington, D.C.: Catholic University
Press, 1921.

Santayana, George. Three Philosophical Poets:
Lucretius, Dante, and Goethe. Garden City, New
York: Doubleday, 1940.

Sayers, Dorothy L. Further Papers on Dante. New York:
Harper, 1957.

_____. Introductory Papers on Dante. New York:
Barnes and Noble, 1969.

Singleton, Charles S. An Essay on the Vita Nuova.
Cambridge: Harvard University Press, 1949.

_____. Dante Studies II: Journey to Beatrice.
Cambridge: Harvard University Press, 1958.

Smith, Herbert W. The Greatness of Dante Alighieri.
Bath: Bath University Press, 1974.

Stambler, Bernard. Dante's Other World: The
Purgatorio as Guide to the Divine Comedy.
New York: New York University Press, 1957.

Swing, Thomas K. The Fragile Leaves of the Sibyl:
Dante's Master Plan. Westminster, Maryland:
Newman Press, 1962.

Taylor, H. O. The Medieval Mind. 4th ed. 2 vols.
Cambridge: Harvard University Press, 1949.

Toynbee, Paget. Dante Alighieri: His Life and Works.
Edited by Charles S. Singleton. New York: Harper
and Row, 1967.

Ullman, Walter. Principles of Government and Politics
in the Middle Ages. London: Methuen, 1961.

Voegelin, Eric. The Ecuminic Age. Volume IV of Order
in History. Baton Rouge: Louisiana State
University Press, 1974.

Vossler, Karl. Medieval Culture: an Introduction to
Dante and His Times. Translated by W. C. Lawton.
2 vols. New York: Harcourt, Brace, 1929.

Whitfield, J. H. Dante and Virgil. Oxford: Blackwell,
1949.

Wicksteed, P. H. Dante and Aquinas. New York: Haskel House, 1971 (c. 1913).

Williams, Charles. The Figure of Beatrice. New York: Noonday Press, 1961.


III. Secondary Sources: Articles


Baldassaro, Lawrence. "Dante the Pilgrim: Everyman as Sinner," Dante Studies, XCII (1974), 63-76.

Barolini, T. "Bertran de Born and Sordello: The Poetry of Politics in Dante's Comedy," PMLA, XCIV (May, 1979), 395-405.

Bernardo, Aldo. "The Three Beasts and Perspective in the Divine Comedy," PMLA, LXXVIII (March, 1963), 15-24.

Berrigan, Joseph R. "Vinculum Pacis: Virgil and Dante," Classical Bulletin, XLIII (February, 1967), 49-53.

Carter, B. B. "Dante's Political Conception," Hibbert Journal, XXXV (July 1937), 568-579.

_____. "Dante's Political Ideas," Review of Politics, V (July, 1943), 339-355.

Cioffari, Vincenzo. "Lectura Dantis: Paradiso VIII," Dante Studies, XC (1972), 93-108.

Costanzo, J. F. "De Monarchia of Dante Alighieri," Thought, XLIII (Spring, 1968), 87-126.

Fletcher, Jefferson B. "Dante's School of the Eagle," Romanic Review, XXII (July, 1931), 191-209.

_____. "The Daughter of the Sun," Romanic Review, XVI (October-December, 1925), 330-340.

Foster, Kenelm. "The Canto of the Damned Popes: Inferno XIX," Dante Studies, LXXXVII (1969), 47-68.

_____. "St. Thomas and Dante," New Blackfrairs, LV (April, 1974), 148-155.

Gilbert, Allan H. "Had Dante Read the Politics of Aristotle?," _PMLA_, XLIII (September, 1928), 602-613.

Harkness, Georgia. "Eschatology in the Great Poets," _Religion in Life_, XXII, No. 1 (1952), 85-99.

Heilbronn, Denise. "Dante's Valley of the Princes," _Dante Studies_, XC (1972), 43-58.

Jones, Charles W. "Carolingian Aesthetics: Why Modular Verse?," _Viator_, VI (1975), 309-340.

_____. "Some Introductory Remarks on Bede's Commenatry on Genesis," _Sacris Etudiri_, XIX (1969-1970), 115-198.

Kaske, R. E. "Dante's Purgatorio XXXII and XXXIII: a Survey of Christian History," _University of Toronto Quarterly_, XLIII (Spring, 1974), 193-217.

Kay, Richard. "Dante's Razor and Gratian's D.XV," _Dante Studies_, Vol. XCVII (1979), 65-95.

_____. "Dante's Unnatural Lawyer: Francesco d'Accorso in Inferno XV," _Studia Gratiana_, XV (1972), 147-200.

_____. "The Sin of Brunetto Latini," _Medieval Studies_, XXXI (1969), 262-286.

Matheson, P. E. "Character and Citizenship in Dante," _Hibbert Journal_, V (July, 1907), 856-878.

Mazzeo, Joseph A. "Light Metaphysics, Dante's Convivio and the Letter to Can Grande Della Scala," _Traditio_, XIV (1958), 191-229.

Montano, Rocco. "Dante and Virgil," _Yale Review_, LX (Summer, 1971), 550-561.

Peters, Edward M. "The Failure of Church and Empire: Paradiso XXX," _Medieval Studies_, XXXIV (1972), 326-335.

Reynolds, Barbara. "Dante and History," _Listener_, LXXIV (July 15, 1965), 83-87.

Scott, J. A. "Politics and Inferno X," _Italian Studies_, XIX (1964), 1-13.

Silverstein, Theodore. "On the Genesis of De Monarchia," Speculum, XIII (July, 1938), 326-349.

Singleton, Charles S. "Dante's Allegory," Speculum, XXV (January, 1950), 78-86.

_____. "Dante's Comedy: The Pattern at the Center," Romanic Review, XLII (October, 1951), 169-177.

Stewart, H. L. "Dante and the Schoolmen," Journal of the History of Ideas, X (June, 1949), 357-373.

Swann, N. E. E. "The Politics of Dante's Divina Commedia," Church Quarterly Review, XV (October, 1927), 50-64.

Truscott, James G. "Ulysses and Guido (Inf. XXVI-XXVII)," Dante Studies, XCI (1973), 47-72.

Ullman, Walter. "The Development of the Medieval Idea of Sovereignty," English Historical Review, LXIV (January, 1949), 1-33.

Walsh, G. "Dante's Philosophy of History," Catholic Historical Review, XX (July, 1934), 117-134.

Williams, Charles. "Religion and Love in Dante," Nottingham Medieval Studies, IX (1965), 50-70.

# Index

142

Judas, 48, 120

Judgment, faculty of, 28, 29, 51, 62, 67, 114, 115, 116

Justice, 6, 45, 119, 123

Justinian, Emperor, 55, 85, 132

Kay, Richard, 42-43

Keys to the Kingdom, 11, 58

Law, 5, 9, 14, 39, 43, 55, 62, 70, 84, 93, 115, 116, 127

Lethe, 73, 75, 89

Letter to Can Grande, 19, 21, 27, 110

Limbo, 34, 37, 38

Lordship, attribute of Emperor, 118

Love, Dante's theory of, 64-67, 78, 88, 114

Lucy, Saint, 33, 109

Man, his nature (two aspects), 12, 112, 131; his two ends, 12, 13, 63, 112, 113, 115, 124; relation of these two ends, 112-114; means by which reached, 112; his eternal end, 14, 59, 79, 112, 116; his temporal end, 14, 55, 59, 72, 73; temporal end really an end in itself, 114; man's natural powers, 71, 76; superiority of eternal to temporal end, 113

Marco Lombardo, 61, 63, 64

Matilda, 70, 72, 73

Mazzeo, Joseph, 18

Monarchy, 6, 7, 8, 11, 13, 17, 53, 63, 64, 83 98, 113, 118

Moore, Edward, 127

Nardi, Bruno, 93

Nero, Emperor, 75

Nino Visconti, 60

Noble Castle, 37, 50, 71

Oderisi, 59

Pageant of Revelation, 73, 75, 76, 120

Paternal standing of the Pope, 118

Paul, Saint, 23, 35

Peace, 6, 9, 13, 55, 57, 58, 78 83, 84, 93, 94, 119

Peter, Saint, 11, 58, 100, 103-106, 121

Peter Damian, Saint, 99, 104

Philosophy, 2, 4, 5, 13, 14, 18, 31, 32, 44, 69, 74, 94

Piccarda Donati, 82, 84

Piero della Vigne, 42

Political life, value of, 15, 17, 18, 22, 74, 91, 92, 100-108, 111, 124, 134

Power (papal) of binding and loosing, 11

Pride, 59, 99

Prime Good, see Supreme Good